ENCYCLICAL LETTER
UT UNUM SINT
OF THE HOLY FATHER
JOHN PAUL II
ON COMMITMENT
TO ECUMENISM

Publication No. 5-050
United States Catholic Conference
Washington, D.C.
ISBN 1-57455-050-0

Text and format from
LIBRERIA EDITRICE VATICANA
VATICAN CITY

CONTENTS

CHAPTER III

QUANTA EST NOBIS VIA?

INTRODUCTION

1.   *UT UNUM SINT!* The call for Christian unity made by the Second Vatican Ecumenical Council with such impassioned commitment is finding an ever greater echo in the hearts of believers, especially as the Year 2000 approaches, a year which Christians will celebrate as a sacred Jubilee, the commemoration of the Incarnation of the Son of God, who became man in order to save humanity.

The courageous witness of so many martyrs of our century, including members of Churches and Ecclesial Communities not in full communion with the Catholic Church, gives new vigour to the Council's call and reminds us of our duty to listen to and put into practice its exhortation. These brothers and sisters of ours, united in the selfless offering of their lives for the Kingdom of God, are the most powerful proof that every factor of division can be transcended and overcome in the total gift of self for the sake of the Gospel.

Christ calls all his disciples to unity. My earnest desire is to renew this call today, to propose it once more with determination, repeating what I said at the Roman Colosseum on Good Friday 1994, at the end of the meditation on the *Via Cru-*

cis prepared by my Venerable Brother Bartholomew, the Ecumenical Patriarch of Constantinople. There I stated that believers in Christ, united in following in the footsteps of the martyrs, cannot remain divided. If they wish truly and effectively to oppose the world's tendency to reduce to powerlessness the Mystery of Redemption, they must *profess together the same truth about the Cross*.[1] The Cross! An anti-Christian outlook seeks to minimize the Cross, to empty it of its meaning, and to deny that in it man has the source of his new life. It claims that the Cross is unable to provide either vision or hope. Man, it says, is nothing but an earthly being, who must live as if God did not exist.

2.   No one is unaware of the challenge which all this poses to believers. They cannot fail to meet this challenge. Indeed, how could they refuse to do everything possible, with God's help, to break down the walls of division and distrust, to overcome obstacles and prejudices which thwart the proclamation of the Gospel of salvation in the Cross of Jesus, the one Redeemer of man, of every individual?

I thank the Lord that he has led us to make progress along the path of unity and communion between Christians, a path difficult but so full of joy. Interconfessional dialogues at the theological level have produced positive and tangible results: this encourages us to move forward.

[1] Cf. Address following the Way of the Cross on Good Friday (1 April 1994), 3: *AAS* 87 (1995), 88.

Nevertheless, besides the doctrinal differences needing to be resolved, Christians cannot underestimate the burden of *long-standing misgivings* inherited from the past, and of mutual *misunderstandings* and *prejudices. Complacency, indifference* and *insufficient knowledge of one another* often make this situation worse. Consequently, the commitment to ecumenism must be based upon the conversion of hearts and upon prayer, which will also lead to the *necessary purification of past memories.* With the grace of the Holy Spirit, the Lord's disciples, inspired by love, by the power of the truth and by a sincere desire for mutual forgiveness and reconciliation, are called to *re-examine together their painful past* and the hurt which that past regrettably continues to provoke even today. All together, they are invited by the ever fresh power of the Gospel to acknowledge with sincere and total objectivity the mistakes made and the contingent factors at work at the origins of their deplorable divisions. *What is needed is a calm, clear-sighted and truthful vision of things,* a vision enlivened by divine mercy and capable of freeing people's minds and of inspiring in everyone a renewed willingness, precisely with a view to proclaiming the Gospel to the men and women of every people and nation.

3.   At the Second Vatican Council, the Catholic Church committed herself *irrevocably* to following the path of the ecumenical venture, thus heeding the Spirit of the Lord, who teaches people to interpret carefully the "signs of the times" . The ex-

periences of these years have made the Church even more profoundly aware of her identity and her mission in history. The Catholic Church acknowledges and confesses *the weaknesses of her members,* conscious that their sins are so many betrayals of and obstacles to the accomplishment of the Saviour's plan. Because she feels herself constantly called to be renewed in the spirit of the Gospel, she does not cease to do penance. At the same time, she acknowledges and exalts still more *the power of the Lord,* who fills her with the gift of holiness, leads her forward, and conforms her to his Passion and Resurrection.

Taught by the events of her history, the Church is committed to freeing herself from every purely human support, in order to live in depth the Gospel law of the Beatitudes. Conscious that the truth does not impose itself except "by virtue of its own truth, as it makes its entrance into the mind at once quietly and with power",[2] she seeks nothing for herself but the freedom to proclaim the Gospel. Indeed, her authority is exercised in the service of truth and charity.

I myself intend *to promote every suitable initiative* aimed at making the witness of the entire Catholic community understood in its full purity and consistency, especially considering the engagement which awaits the Church at the threshold of the new Millennium. That will be an exceptional occasion, in view of which she asks the Lord to in-

[2] SECOND VATICAN ECUMENICAL COUNCIL, Declaration on Religious Freedom *Dignitatis Humanæ*, 1.

crease the unity of all Christians until they reach full communion.[3] The present Encyclical Letter is meant as a contribution to this most noble goal. Essentially pastoral in character, it seeks to encourage the efforts of all who work for the cause of unity.

4.   This is a specific duty of the Bishop of Rome as the Successor of the Apostle Peter. I carry out this duty with the profound conviction that I am obeying the Lord, and with a clear sense of my own human frailty. Indeed, if Christ himself gave Peter this special mission in the Church and exhorted him to strengthen his brethren, he also made clear to him his human weakness and his special need of conversion: "And when you have turned again, strengthen your brethren" (*Lk* 22:32). It is precisely in Peter's human weakness that it becomes fully clear that the Pope, in order to carry out this special ministry in the Church, depends totally on the Lord's grace and prayer: "I have prayed for you that your faith may not fail" (*Lk* 22:32). The conversion of Peter and that of his Successors is upheld by the very prayer of the Redeemer, and the Church constantly makes this petition her own. In our ecumenical age, marked by the Second Vatican Council, the mission of the Bishop of Rome is particularly directed to recalling the need for full communion among Christ's disciples.

[3] Cf. Apostolic Letter *Tertio Millennio Adveniente* (10 November 1994), 16: *AAS* 87 (1995), 15.

The Bishop of Rome himself must fervently make his own Christ's prayer for that conversion which is indispensable for "Peter" to be able to serve his brethren. I earnestly invite the faithful of the Catholic Church and all Christians to share in this prayer. May all join me in praying for this conversion!

We know that during her earthly pilgrimage the Church has suffered and will continue to suffer opposition and persecution. But the hope which sustains her is unshakable, just as the joy which flows from this hope is indestructible. In effect, the firm and enduring rock upon which she is founded is Jesus Christ, her Lord.

CHAPTER I

THE CATHOLIC CHURCH'S COMMITMENT TO ECUMENISM

God's plan and communion

5.   Together with all Christ's disciples, the Catholic Church bases upon God's plan her ecumenical commitment to gather all Christians into unity. Indeed, "the Church is not a reality closed in on herself. Rather, she is permanently open to missionary and ecumenical endeavour, for she is sent to the world to announce and witness, to make present and spread the mystery of communion which is essential to her, and to gather all people and all things into Christ, so as to be for all an 'inseparable sacrament of unity' ".[4]

Already in the Old Testament, the Prophet Ezekiel, referring to the situation of God's People at that time, and using the simple sign of two broken sticks which are first divided and then joined together, expressed the divine will to "gather from all sides" the members of his scattered people. "I will be their God, and they shall be my people. Then the nations will know that I the Lord sancti-

---

[4] CONGREGATION FOR THE DOCTRINE OF THE FAITH, Letter to the Bishops of the Catholic Church on Some Aspects of the Church Understood as Communion *Communionis Notio* (28 May 1992), 4: *AAS* 85 (1993), 840.

fy Israel" (cf. 37:16-28). The Gospel of John, for its part, considering the situation of the People of God at the time it was written, sees in Jesus' death the reason for the unity of God's children: "Jesus would die for the nation, and not for the nation only, but to gather into one the children of God who are scattered abroad" (11:51-52). Indeed, as the Letter to the Ephesians explains, Jesus "broke down the dividing wall of hostility ... through the Cross, thereby bringing the hostility to an end"; in place of what was divided he brought about unity (cf. 2:14-16).

6.   The unity of all divided humanity is the will of God. For this reason he sent his Son, so that by dying and rising for us he might bestow on us the Spirit of love. On the eve of his sacrifice on the Cross, Jesus himself prayed to the Father for his disciples and for all those who believe in him, that they *might be one*, a living communion. This is the basis not only of the duty, but also of the responsibility before God and his plan, which falls to those who through Baptism become members of the Body of Christ, a Body in which the fullness of reconciliation and communion must be made present. How is it possible to remain divided, if we have been "buried" through Baptism in the Lord's death, in the very act by which God, through the death of his Son, has broken down the walls of division? Division "openly contradicts the will of Christ, provides a stumbling block to the world, and inflicts damage on the most holy

cause of proclaiming the Good News to every creature".[5]

The way of ecumenism: the way of the Church

7.　"The Lord of the Ages wisely and patiently follows out the plan of his grace on behalf of us sinners. In recent times he has begun to bestow more generously upon divided Christians remorse over their divisions and a longing for unity. Everywhere, large numbers have felt the impulse of this grace, and among our separated brethren also *there increases from day to day a movement,* fostered by the grace of the Holy Spirit, *for the restoration of unity among all Christians.* Taking part in this movement, which is called ecumenical, are those who invoke the Triune God and confess Jesus as Lord and Saviour. They join in not merely as individuals but also as members of the corporate groups in which they have heard the Gospel, and which each regards as his Church and, indeed, God's. And yet almost everyone, though in different ways, *longs that there may be one visible Church of God,* a Church truly universal and sent forth to the whole world that the world may be converted to the Gospel and so be saved, to the glory of God".[6]

8.　This statement of the Decree *Unitatis Redintegratio* is to be read in the context of the com-

---

[5] SECOND VATICAN ECUMENICAL COUNCIL, Decree on Ecumenism *Unitatis Redintegratio*, 1.
[6] *Ibid.*

plete teaching of the Second Vatican Council. The Council expresses the Church's decision to take up the ecumenical task of working for Christian unity and to propose it with conviction and vigour: "This sacred Synod exhorts all the Catholic faithful to recognize the signs of the times and to participate actively in the work of ecumenism".[7]

In indicating the Catholic principles of ecumenism, the Decree *Unitatis Redintegratio* recalls above all the teaching on the Church set forth in the Dogmatic Constitution *Lumen Gentium* in its chapter on the People of God.[8] At the same time, it takes into account everything affirmed in the Council's Declaration on Religious Freedom *Dignitatis Humanae*.[9]

The Catholic Church embraces with hope the commitment to ecumenism as a duty of the Christian conscience enlightened by faith and guided by love. Here too we can apply the words of Saint Paul to the first Christians of Rome: "God's love has been poured into our hearts through the Holy Spirit"; thus our "hope does not disappoint us" (*Rom* 5:5). This is the hope of Christian unity, which has its divine source in the Trinitarian unity of the Father, the Son and the Holy Spirit.

9.   Jesus himself, at the hour of his Passion, prayed "that they may all be one" (*Jn* 17:21). This

[7] *Ibid.*, 4.
[8] Cf. SECOND VATICAN ECUMENICAL COUNCIL, Dogmatic Constitution on the Church *Lumen Gentium*, 14.
[9] Cf. SECOND VATICAN ECUMENICAL COUNCIL, Declaration on Religious Freedom *Dignitatis Humanæ*, 1 and 2.

unity, which the Lord has bestowed on his Church and in which he wishes to embrace all people, is not something added on, but stands at the very heart of Christ's mission. Nor is it some secondary attribute of the community of his disciples. Rather, it belongs to the very essence of this community. God wills the Church, because he wills unity, and unity is an expression of the whole depth of his *agape*.

In effect, this unity bestowed by the Holy Spirit does not merely consist in the gathering of people as a collection of individuals. It is a unity constituted by the bonds of the profession of faith, the sacraments and hierarchical communion.[10] The faithful are *one* because, in the Spirit, they are in *communion* with the Son and, in him, share in his *communion* with the Father: "Our *fellowship* is with the Father and with his Son Jesus Christ" (1 *Jn* 1:3). For the Catholic Church, then, the *communion* of Christians is none other than the manifestation in them of the grace by which God makes them sharers in his own *communion*, which is his eternal life. Christ's words "that they may be one" are thus his prayer to the Father that the Father's plan may be fully accomplished, in such a way that everyone may clearly see "what is the plan of the mystery hidden for ages in God who created all things" (*Eph* 3:9). To believe in Christ means to desire unity; to desire unity means to desire the Church; to desire the Church means to

<hr />

[10] Cf. SECOND VATICAN ECUMENICAL COUNCIL, Dogmatic Constitution on the Church *Lumen Gentium*, 14.

desire the communion of grace which corresponds to the Father's plan from all eternity. Such is the meaning of Christ's prayer: *"Ut unum sint"*.

10.　　In the present situation of the lack of unity among Christians and of the confident quest for full communion, the Catholic faithful are conscious of being deeply challenged by the Lord of the Church. The Second Vatican Council strengthened their commitment with a clear ecclesiological vision, open to all the ecclesial values present among other Christians. The Catholic faithful face the ecumenical question in a spirit of faith.

The Council states that the Church of Christ "subsists in the Catholic Church, which is governed by the Successor of Peter and by the Bishops in communion with him", and at the same time acknowledges that "many elements of sanctification and of truth can be found outside her visible structure. These elements, however, as gifts properly belonging to the Church of Christ, possess an inner dynamism towards Catholic unity".[11]

"It follows that these separated Churches and Communities, though we believe that they suffer from defects, have by no means been deprived of significance and value in the mystery of salvation. For the Spirit of Christ has not refrained from using them as means of salvation which derive their efficacy from the very fullness of grace and truth entrusted to the Catholic Church".[12]

[11] *Ibid.*, 8.
[12] SECOND VATICAN ECUMENICAL COUNCIL, Decree on Ecumenism *Unitatis Redintegratio*, 3.

11.   The Catholic Church thus affirms that during the two thousand years of her history she has been preserved in unity, with all the means with which God wishes to endow his Church, and this despite the often grave crises which have shaken her, the infidelity of some of her ministers, and the faults into which her members daily fall. The Catholic Church knows that, by virtue of the strength which comes to her from the Spirit, the weaknesses, mediocrity, sins and at times the betrayals of some of her children cannot destroy what God has bestowed on her as part of his plan of grace. Moreover, "the powers of death shall not prevail against it" (*Mt* 16:18). Even so, the Catholic Church does not forget that many among her members cause God's plan to be discernible only with difficulty. Speaking of the lack of unity among Christians, the Decree on Ecumenism does not ignore the fact that "people of both sides were to blame",[13] and acknowledges that responsibility cannot be attributed only to the "other side". By God's grace, however, neither what belongs to the structure of the Church of Christ nor that communion which still exists with the other Churches and Ecclesial Communities has been destroyed.

Indeed, the elements of sanctification and truth present in the other Christian Communities, in a degree which varies from one to the other, constitute the objective basis of the communion, albeit imperfect, which exists between them and the Catholic Church.

[13] *Ibid.*

15

To the extent that these elements are found in other Christian Communities, the one Church of Christ is effectively present in them. For this reason the Second Vatican Council speaks of a certain, though imperfect communion. The Dogmatic Constitution *Lumen Gentium* stresses that the Catholic Church "recognizes that in many ways she is linked" [14] with these Communities by a true union in the Holy Spirit.

12.   The same Dogmatic Constitution listed at length "the elements of sanctification and truth" which in various ways are present and operative beyond the visible boundaries of the Catholic Church: "For there are many who honour Sacred Scripture, taking it as a norm of belief and of action, and who show a true religious zeal. They lovingly believe in God the Father Almighty and in Christ, Son of God and Saviour. They are consecrated by Baptism, through which they are united with Christ. They also recognize and receive other sacraments within their own Churches or Ecclesial Communities. Many of them rejoice in the episcopate, celebrate the Holy Eucharist, and cultivate devotion towards the Virgin Mother of God. They also share with us in prayer and other spiritual itual benefits. Likewise, we can say that in some real way they are joined with us in the Holy Spirit, for to them also he gives his gifts and graces, and is thereby operative among them with his sanctifying power. Some indeed he has

[14] No. 15.

strengthened to the extent of the shedding of their blood. In all of Christ's disciples the Spirit arouses the desire to be peacefully united, in the manner determined by Christ, as one flock under one shepherd".[15]

The Council's Decree on Ecumenism, referring to the Orthodox Churches, went so far as to declare that "through the celebration of the Eucharist of the Lord in each of these Churches, the Church of God is built up and grows in stature".[16] Truth demands that all this be recognized.

13.   The same Document carefully draws out the doctrinal implications of this situation. Speaking of the members of these Communities, it declares: "All those justified by faith through Baptism are incorporated into Christ. They therefore have a right to be honoured by the title of Christian, and are properly regarded as brothers and sisters in the Lord by the sons and daughters of the Catholic Church".[17]

With reference to the many positive elements present in the other Churches and Ecclesial Communities, the Decree adds: "All of these, which come from Christ and lead back to him, belong by right to the one Church of Christ. The separated brethren also carry out many of the sacred actions of the Christian religion. Undoubtedly, in many ways that vary according to the condition of each

[15] *Ibid.*
[16] SECOND VATICAN ECUMENICAL COUNCIL, Decree on Ecumenism *Unitatis Redintegratio*, 15.
[17] *Ibid.*, 3.

Church or Community, these actions can truly engender a life of grace, and can be rightly described as capable of providing access to the community of salvation".[18]

These are extremely important texts for ecumenism. It is not that beyond the boundaries of the Catholic community there is an ecclesial vacuum. Many elements of great value (*eximia*), which in the Catholic Church are part of the fullness of the means of salvation and of the gifts of grace which make up the Church, are also found in the other Christian Communities.

14.   All these elements bear within themselves a tendency towards unity, having their fullness in that unity. It is not a matter of adding together all the riches scattered throughout the various Christian Communities in order to arrive at a Church which God has in mind for the future. In accordance with the great Tradition, attested to by the Fathers of the East and of the West, the Catholic Church believes that in the Pentecost Event God has *already* manifested the Church in her eschatological reality, which he had prepared "from the time of Abel, the just one".[19] This reality is something already given. Consequently we are even now in the last times. The elements of this already-given Church exist, found in their fullness

---

[18] *Ibid.*

[19] Cf. SAINT GREGORY THE GREAT, *Homilies on the Gospel*, 19, 1: *PL*, 1154, quoted in SECOND VATICAN ECUMENICAL COUNCIL, Dogmatic Constitution on the Church *Lumen Gentium*, 2.

in the Catholic Church and, without this fullness, in the other Communities,[20] where certain features of the Christian mystery have at times been more effectively emphasized. Ecumenism is directed precisely to making the partial communion existing between Christians grow towards full communion in truth and charity.

Renewal and conversion

15.   Passing from principles, from the obligations of the Christian conscience, to the actual practice of the ecumenical journey towards unity, the Second Vatican Council emphasizes above all *the need for interior conversion.* The messianic proclamation that "the time is fulfilled and the Kingdom of God is at hand", and the subsequent call to "repent, and believe in the Gospel" (*Mk* 1:15) with which Jesus begins his mission, indicate the essential element of every new beginning: the fundamental need for evangelization at every stage of the Church's journey of salvation. This is true in a special way of the process begun by the Second Vatican Council, when it indicated as a dimension of renewal the ecumenical task of uniting divided Christians. *"There can be no ecumenism worthy of the name without a change of heart".*[21]

The Council calls for personal conversion as well as for communal conversion. The desire of

---

[20] Cf. SECOND VATICAN ECUMENICAL COUNCIL, Decree on Ecumenism *Unitatis Redintegratio*, 4.
[21] *Ibid.*, 7.

every Christian Community for unity goes hand in hand with its fidelity to the Gospel. In the case of individuals who live their Christian vocation, the Council speaks of interior conversion, of a renewal of mind.[22]

Each one therefore ought to be more radically converted to the Gospel and, without ever losing sight of God's plan, change his or her way of looking at things. Thanks to ecumenism, our contemplation of "the mighty works of God" (*mirabilia Dei*) has been enriched by new horizons, for which the Triune God calls us to give thanks: the knowledge that the Spirit is at work in other Christian Communities, the discovery of examples of holiness, the experience of the immense riches present in the communion of saints, and contact with unexpected dimensions of Christian commitment. In a corresponding way, there is an increased sense of the need for repentance: an awareness of certain exclusions which seriously harm fraternal charity, of certain refusals to forgive, of a certain pride, of an unevangelical insistence on condemning the "other side", of a disdain born of an unhealthy presumption. Thus, the entire life of Christians is marked by a concern for ecumenism; and they are called to let themselves be shaped, as it were, by that concern.

16.   In the teaching of the Second Vatican Council there is a clear connection between renewal, conversion and reform. The Council states that "Christ summons the Church, as she goes her

[22] Cf. *ibid.*

pilgrim way, to that continual reformation of which she always has need, insofar as she is an institution of human beings here on earth. Therefore, if the influence of events or of the times has led to deficiencies ... these should be appropriately rectified at the proper moment".[23] No Christian Community can exempt itself from this call.

By engaging in frank dialogue, Communities help one another to look at themselves together in the light of the Apostolic Tradition. This leads them to ask themselves whether they truly express in an adequate way all that the Holy Spirit has transmitted through the Apostles.[24] With regard to the Catholic Church, I have frequently recalled these obligations and perspectives, as for example on the anniversary of the *Baptism of Kievan Rus'* [25] or in commemorating the eleven hundred years since the evangelizing activity of Saints Cyril and Methodius.[26] More recently, the *Directory for the Application of Principles and Norms on Ecumenism*, issued with my approval by the Pontifical Council for Promoting Christian Unity, has applied them to the pastoral sphere.[27]

17.   With regard to other Christians, the principal documents of the Commission on *Faith and*

[23] *Ibid.*, 6.

[24] Cf. SECOND VATICAN ECUMENICAL COUNCIL, Dogmatic Constitution *Dei Verbum*, 7.

[25] Cf. Apostolic Letter *Euntes in Mundum* (25 January 1988): *AAS* 80 (1988), 935-956.

[26] Cf. Encyclical Epistle *Slavorum Apostoli* (2 June 1985): *AAS* 77 (1985), 779-813.

[27] Cf. *Directory for the Application of Principles and Norms on Ecumenism* (25 March 1993): *AAS* 85 (1993), 1039-1119.

Order [28] and the statements of numerous bilateral dialogues have already provided Christian Communities with useful tools for discerning what is necessary to the ecumenical movement and to the conversion which it must inspire. These studies are important from two points of view: they demonstrate the remarkable progress already made, and they are a source of hope inasmuch as they represent a sure foundation for further study.

The increase of fellowship in a reform which is continuous and carried out in the light of the Apostolic Tradition is certainly, in the present circumstances of Christians, one of the distinctive and most important aspects of ecumenism. Moreover, it is an essential guarantee for its future. The faithful of the Catholic Church cannot forget that the ecumenical thrust of the Second Vatican Council is one consequence of all that the Church at that time committed herself to doing in order to re-examine herself in the light of the Gospel and the great Tradition. My Predecessor, Pope John XXIII, understood this clearly: in calling the Council, he refused to separate renewal from ecumenical openness.[29] At the conclusion of the Council, Pope Paul VI solemnly sealed the Council's commitment to ecumenism, renewing the dialogue of charity with the Churches in communion with

---

[28] Cf. in particular, the Lima Document: *Baptism, Eucharist and Ministry* (January 1982); and the study of the JOINT WORKING GROUP BETWEEN THE CATHOLIC CHURCH AND THE WORLD COUNCIL OF CHURCHES, *Confessing the "One" Faith* (1991), Document No. 153 of the Commission on Faith and Order, Geneva, 1991.

[29] Cf. Opening Address of the Second Vatican Ecumenical Council (11 October 1962): *AAS* 54 (1962), 793.

the Patriarch of Constantinople, and joining the Patriarch in the concrete and profoundly significant gesture which "condemned to oblivion" and "removed from memory and from the midst of the Church" the excommunications of the past. It is worth recalling that the establishment of a special body for ecumenical matters coincided with the launching of preparations for the Second Vatican Council [30] and that through this body the opinions and judgments of the other Christian Communities played a part in the great debates about Revelation, the Church, the nature of ecumenism and religious freedom.

The fundamental importance of doctrine

18.   Taking up an idea expressed by Pope John XXIII at the opening of the Council,[31] the Decree on Ecumenism mentions the way of formulating doctrine as one of the elements of a continuing reform.[32] Here it is not a question of altering the deposit of faith, changing the meaning of dogmas,

---

[30] We are speaking of the SECRETARIAT FOR PROMOTING CHRISTIAN UNITY, established by Pope John XXIII with the Motu Proprio *Superno Dei Nutu* (5 June 1960), 9: *AAS* 52 (1960), 436, and confirmed by successive documents: JOHN XXIII Motu Proprio *Appropinquante Concilio* (6 August 1962), c. III, a. 7, § 2, I: *AAS* 54 (1962), 614; cf. PAUL VI Apostolic Constitution *Regimini Ecclesiae Universae* (15 August 1967), 92-94: *AAS* 59 (1967), 918-919. This dicastery is now called the PONTIFICAL COUNCIL FOR PROMOTING CHRISTIAN UNITY: cf. JOHN PAUL II, Apostolic Constitution *Pastor Bonus* (28 June 1988), V, Arts. 135-138: *AAS* 80 (1988), 895-896.
[31] Opening Address of the Second Vatican Ecumenical Council (11 October 1962): *AAS* 54 (1962), 792.
[32] Cf. SECOND VATICAN ECUMENICAL COUNCIL, Decree on Ecumenism *Unitatis Redintegratio*, 6.

eliminating essential words from them, accommodating truth to the preferences of a particular age, or suppressing certain articles of the *Creed* under the false pretext that they are no longer understood today. The unity willed by God can be attained only by the adherence of all to the content of revealed faith in its entirety. In matters of faith, compromise is in contradiction with God who is Truth. In the Body of Christ, "the way, and the truth, and the life" (*Jn* 14:6), who could consider legitimate a reconciliation brought about at the expense of the truth? The Council's Declaration on Religious Freedom *Dignitatis Humanae* attributes to human dignity the quest for truth, "especially in what concerns God and his Church",[33] and adherence to truth's demands. A "being together" which betrayed the truth would thus be opposed both to the nature of God who offers his communion and to the need for truth found in the depths of every human heart.

19.   Even so, doctrine needs to be presented in a way that makes it understandable to those for whom God himself intends it. In my Encyclical Epistle *Slavorum Apostoli*, I recalled that this was the very reason why Saints Cyril and Methodius laboured to translate the ideas of the Bible and the concepts of Greek theology in the context of very different historical experiences and ways of thinking. They wanted the one word of God to be "made accessible in each civilization's own forms

[33] SECOND VATICAN ECUMENICAL COUNCIL, Declaration on Religious Freedom *Dignitatis Humanæ*, 1.

of expression".[34] They recognized that they could not therefore "impose on the peoples assigned to their preaching either the undeniable superiority of the Greek language and Byzantine culture, or the customs and way of life of the more advanced society in which they had grown up".[35] Thus they put into practice that "perfect communion in love which preserves the Church from all forms of particularism, ethnic exclusivism or racial prejudice, and from any nationalistic arrogance".[36] In the same spirit, I did not hesitate to say to the Aboriginal Peoples of Australia: "You do not have to be divided into two parts ... Jesus calls you to accept his words and his values into your own culture".[37] Because by its nature the content of faith is meant for all humanity, it must be translated into all cultures. Indeed, the element which determines communion in truth is *the meaning of truth*. The expression of truth can take different forms. The renewal of these forms of expression becomes necessary for the sake of transmitting to the people of today the Gospel message in its unchanging meaning.[38]

"This renewal therefore has notable ecumenical significance".[39] And not only renewal in which

[34] Encyclical Epistle *Slavorum Apostoli* (2 June 1985), 11: *AAS* 77 (1985), 792.

[35] *Ibid.*, 13: *loc. cit.*, 794.

[36] *Ibid.*, 11: *loc. cit.*, 792.

[37] Address to the Aboriginal Peoples (29 November 1986), 12: *AAS* 79 (1987), 977.

[38] Cf. SAINT VINCENT OF LERINS, *Commonitorium primum*, 23: *PL* 50, 667-668.

[39] SECOND VATICAN ECUMENICAL COUNCIL, Decree on Ecumenism *Unitatis Redintegratio*, 6.

the faith is expressed, but also of the very life of faith. It might therefore be asked: who is responsible for doing this? To this question the Council replies clearly: "Concern for restoring unity pertains to the whole Church, faithful and clergy alike. It extends to everyone, according to the ability of each, whether it be exercised in daily Christian living or in theological and historical studies".[40]

20.   All this is extremely important and of fundamental significance for ecumenical activity. Thus it is absolutely clear that ecumenism, the movement promoting Christian unity, *is not just some sort of "appendix"* which is added to the Church's traditional activity. Rather, ecumenism is an organic part of her life and work, and consequently must pervade all that she is and does; it must be like the fruit borne by a healthy and flourishing tree which grows to its full stature.

This is what Pope John XIII believed about the unity of the Church and how he saw full Christian unity. With regard to other Christians, to the great Christian family, he observed: "What unites us is much greater than what divides us". The Second Vatican Council for its part exhorts "all Christ's faithful to remember that the more purely they strive to live according to the Gospel, the more they are fostering and even practising Christian unity. For they can achieve depth and ease in strengthening mutual brotherhood to the

[40] *Ibid.*, 5.

degree that they enjoy profound communion with the Father, the Word, and the Holy Spirit".[41]

The primacy of prayer

21.   "This *change of heart and holiness of life, along with public and private prayer for the unity of Christians*, should be regarded as the soul of the whole ecumenical movement, and can rightly be called 'spiritual ecumenism' ".[42]

We proceed along the road leading to the conversion of hearts guided by love which is directed to God and, at the same time, to all our brothers and sisters, including those not in full communion with us. Love gives rise to the desire for unity, even in those who have never been aware of the need for it. Love builds communion between individuals and between Communities. If we love one another, we strive to deepen our communion and make it perfect. *Love is given to God* as the perfect source of communion—the unity of Father, Son and Holy Spirit—that we may draw from that source the strength to build communion between individuals and Communities, or to re-establish it between Christians still divided. Love is the great undercurrent which gives life and adds vigour to the movement towards unity.

This love *finds its most complete expression in common prayer*. When brothers and sisters who are not in perfect communion with one another

[41] *Ibid.*, 7.
[42] *Ibid.*, 8.

come together to pray, the Second Vatican Council defines their prayer as *the soul of the whole ecumenical movement*. This prayer is "a very effective means of petitioning for the grace of unity", "a *genuine expression of the ties which even now bind Catholics to their separated brethren*".[43] Even when prayer is not specifically offered for Christian unity, but for other intentions such as peace, it actually becomes an expression and confirmation of unity. The common prayer of Christians is an invitation to Christ himself to visit the community of those who call upon him: "Where two or three are gathered in my name, there am I in the midst of them" (*Mt* 18:20).

22.   When Christians pray together, the goal of unity seems closer. The long history of Christians marked by many divisions seems to converge once more because it tends towards that Source of its unity which is Jesus Christ. He "is the same yesterday, today and forever!" (*Heb* 13:8). In the fellowship of prayer Christ is truly present; he prays "in us", "with us" and "for us". It is he who leads our prayer in the Spirit-Consoler whom he promised and then bestowed on his Church in the Upper Room in Jerusalem, when he established her in her original unity.

Along the ecumenical path to unity, pride of place certainly belongs to *common prayer*, the prayerful union of those who gather together around Christ himself. If Christians, despite their

---

[43] *Ibid.*

divisions, can grow ever more united in common prayer around Christ, they will grow in the awareness of how little divides them in comparison to what unites them. If they meet more often and more regularly before Christ in prayer, they will be able to gain the courage to face all the painful human reality of their divisions, and they will find themselves together once more in that community of the Church which Christ constantly builds up in the Holy Spirit, in spite of all weaknesses and human limitations.

23. Finally, *fellowship in prayer leads people to look at the Church and Christianity in a new way.* It must not be forgotten in fact that the Lord prayed to the Father that his disciples might be one, so that their unity might bear witness to his mission and the world would believe that the Father had sent him (cf. *Jn* 17:21). It can be said that the ecumenical movement in a certain sense was born out of the negative experience of each one of those who, in proclaiming the one Gospel, appealed to his own Church or Ecclesial Community. This was a contradiction which could not escape those who listened to the message of salvation and found in this fact an obstacle to acceptance of the Gospel. Regrettably, this grave obstacle has not been overcome. It is true that we are not yet in full communion. And yet, despite our divisions, we are on the way towards full unity, that unity which marked the Apostolic Church at its birth and which we sincerely seek. Our common prayer, inspired by faith, is proof of this. In that prayer, we gather

together in the name of Christ who is One. He is our unity.

"Ecumenical" prayer is at the service of the Christian mission and its credibility. It must thus be especially present in the life of the Church and in every activity aimed at fostering Christian unity. It is as if we constantly need to go back and meet in the Upper Room of Holy Thursday, even though our presence together in that place will not be perfect until the obstacles to full ecclesial communion are overcome and all Christians can gather together in the common celebration of the Eucharist.[44]

24.   It is a source of joy to see that the many ecumenical meetings almost always include and indeed culminate in prayer. The *Week of Prayer for Christian Unity*, celebrated in January or, in some countries, around Pentecost, has become a widespread and well established tradition. But there are also many other occasions during the year when Christians are led to pray together. In this context, I wish to mention the special experience of the *Pope's pilgrimages to the various Churches* in the different continents and countries of the present-day *oikoumene*. I am very conscious that it was the Second Vatican Council which led the Pope to exercise his apostolic ministry in this particular way. Even more can be said. The Council made these visits of the Pope a specific responsibility in carrying out the role of the Bishop of

[44] Cf. *ibid.*, 4.

Rome at the service of communion.[45] My visits have almost always included an ecumenical meeting and *common prayer with our brothers and sisters who seek unity in Christ and in his Church*. With profound emotion I remember praying together with the Primate of the Anglican Communion at Canterbury Cathedral (29 May 1982); in that magnificent edifice, I saw "an eloquent witness *both to our long years of common inheritance and to the sad years of division that followed*".[46] Nor can I forget the meetings held in the Scandinavian and Nordic Countries (1-10 June 1989), in North and South America and in Africa, and at the headquarters of the World Council of Churches (12 June 1984), the organization committed to calling its member Churches and Ecclesial Communities "to the goal of visible unity in one faith and in one Eucharistic fellowship expressed in worship and in common life in Christ".[47] And how could I ever forget taking part in the Eucharistic Liturgy in the Church of Saint George at the Ecumenical Patriarchate (30 November 1979), and the service held in Saint Peter's Basilica during the visit to Rome of my Venerable Brother, Patriarch Dimitrios I (6 December 1987)? On that occasion, at the Altar of the Confession, we recited together the Nicene-Constantinopolitan Creed according to its original Greek text. It is hard to describe in

[45] Cf. JOHN PAUL II, Apostolic Letter *Tertio Millennio Adveniente* (10 November 1994), 24: *AAS* 87 (1995), 19-20.

[46] Address at Canterbury Cathedral (29 May 1982), 5: *AAS* 74 (1982), 922.

[47] WORLD COUNCIL OF CHURCHES, *Constitution and Rules*, III, 1.

a few words the unique nature of each of these occasions of prayer. Given the differing ways in which each of these meetings was conditioned by past events, each had its own special eloquence. They have all become part of the Church's memory as she is guided by the Paraclete to seek the full unity of all believers in Christ.

25.   It is not just the Pope who has become a pilgrim. In recent years, many distinguished leaders of other Churches and Ecclesial Communities have visited me in Rome, and I have been able to join them in prayer, both in public and in private. I have already mentioned the visit of the Ecumenical Patriarch Dimitrios I. I would now like to recall the prayer meeting, also held in Saint Peter's Basilica, at which I joined the Lutheran Archbishops, the Primates of Sweden and Finland, for the celebration of Vespers on the occasion of the Sixth Centenary of the Canonization of Saint Birgitta (5 October 1991). This is just one example, because awareness of the duty to pray for unity has become an integral part of the Church's life. There is no important or significant event which does not benefit from Christians coming together and praying. It is impossible for me to give a complete list of such meetings, even though each one deserves to be mentioned. Truly the Lord has taken us by the hand and is guiding us. These exchanges and these prayers have already written pages and pages of our "Book of unity", a "Book" which we must constantly return to and re-read so as to draw from it new inspiration and hope.

26.   Prayer, the community at prayer, enables us always to discover anew the evangelical truth of the words: *"You have one Father"* (Mt 23:9), the Father—*Abba*—invoked by Christ himself, the Only-begotten and Consubstantial Son. And again: *"You have one teacher*, and *you are all brethren"* (*Mt* 23:8). "Ecumenical" prayer discloses this fundamental dimension of brotherhood in Christ, who died to gather together the children of God who were scattered, so that in becoming "sons and daughters in the Son" (cf. *Eph* 1:5) we might show forth more fully both the mysterious reality of God's fatherhood and the truth about the human nature shared by each and every individual.

"Ecumenical" prayer, as the prayer of brothers and sisters, expresses all this. Precisely because they are separated from one another, they *meet in Christ* with all the more hope, *entrusting to him the future of their unity and their communion.* Here too we can appropriately apply the teaching of the Council: "The Lord Jesus, when he prayed to the Father *'that all may be one ... as we are one'* (*Jn* 17:21-22), opened up vistas closed to human reason. For he implied a certain likeness between the union of the Divine Persons, and the union of God's children in truth and charity".[48]

The change of heart which is the essential condition for every authentic search for unity flows from prayer and its realization is guided by

---

[48] SECOND VATICAN ECUMENICAL COUNCIL, Pastoral Constitution on the Church in the Modern World *Gaudium et Spes*, 24.

prayer: "For it is from newness of attitudes, from self-denial and unstinted love, that yearnings for unity take their rise and grow towards maturity. We should therefore *pray to the divine Spirit* for the grace to be genuinely self-denying, humble, gentle in the service of others, and to have an attitude of brotherly generosity towards them".[49]

27.   Praying for unity is not a matter reserved only to those who actually experience the lack of unity among Christians. In the deep personal dialogue which each of us must carry on with the Lord in prayer, concern for unity cannot be absent. Only in this way, in fact, will that concern fully become part of the reality of our life and of the commitments we have taken on in the Church. It was in order to reaffirm this duty that I set before the faithful of the Catholic Church a model which I consider exemplary, the model of a Trappistine Sister, *Blessed Maria Gabriella of Unity*, whom I beatified on 25 January 1983.[50] Sister Maria Gabriella, called by her vocation to be apart from the world, devoted her life to meditation and prayer centered on chapter seventeen of Saint John's Gospel, and offered her life for Christian unity. This is truly the cornerstone of all prayer:

---

[49] SECOND VATICAN ECUMENICAL COUNCIL, Decree on Ecumenism *Unitatis Redintegratio*, 7.

[50] Maria Sagheddu was born at Dorgali (Sardinia) in 1914. At twenty-one years of age she entered the Trappistine Monastery in Grottaferrata. Through the apostolic labours of Abbé Paul Couturier, she came to understand the need for prayers and spiritual sacrifices for the unity of Christians. In 1936, at the time of an *Octave for Unity,* she chose to offer her life for the unity of the Church. Following a grave illness, Sister Maria Gabriella died on 23 April 1939.

the total and unconditional offering of one's life to the Father, through the Son, in the Holy Spirit. The example of Sister Maria Gabriella is instructive; it helps us to understand that there are no special times, situations or places of prayer for unity. Christ's prayer to the Father is offered as a model for everyone, always and everywhere.

Ecumenical dialogue

28.   If prayer is the "soul" of ecumenical renewal and of the yearning for unity, it is the basis and support for *everything the Council defines as "dialogue"*. This definition is certainly not unrelated to today's *personalist way of thinking*. The capacity for "dialogue" is rooted in the nature of the person and his dignity. As seen by philosophy, this approach is linked to the Christian truth concerning man as expressed by the Council: man is in fact "the only creature on earth which God willed for itself"; thus he cannot "fully find himself except through a sincere gift of himself".[51] Dialogue is an indispensable step along the path *towards human self-realization*, the self-realization both of *each individual* and *of every human community*. Although the concept of "dialogue" might appear to give priority to the cognitive dimension (*dia-logos*), all dialogue implies a global, existential dimension. It involves the human subject in his or

---

[51] SECOND VATICAN ECUMENICAL COUNCIL, Pastoral Constitution on the Church in the Modern World *Gaudium et Spes*, 24.

her entirety; dialogue between communities involves in a particular way the subjectivity of each.

This truth about dialogue, so profoundly expressed by Pope Paul VI in his Encyclical *Ecclesiam Suam*,[52] was also taken up by the Council in its teaching and ecumenical activity. Dialogue is not simply an exchange of ideas. In some way it is always an "exchange of gifts".[53]

29.   For this reason, the Council's Decree on Ecumenism also emphasizes the importance of "every effort to eliminate words, judgments, and actions which do not respond to the condition of separated brethren with truth and fairness and so make mutual relations between them more difficult".[54] The Decree approaches the question from the standpoint of the Catholic Church and refers to the criteria which she must apply in relation to other Christians. In all this, however, reciprocity is required. To follow these criteria is a commitment of each of the parties which desire to enter into dialogue and it is a precondition for starting such dialogue. It is necessary to pass from antagonism and conflict to a situation where each party recognizes the other as a *partner*. When undertaking dialogue, *each side must presuppose in the other a desire for reconciliation*, for *unity in truth*. For this to happen, any display of mutual opposition must

    [52] Cf. *AAS* 56 (1964), 609-659.
    [53] Cf. SECOND VATICAN ECUMENICAL COUNCIL, Dogmatic Constitution on the Church *Lumen Gentium*, 13.
    [54] SECOND VATICAN ECUMENICAL COUNCIL, Decree on Ecumenism *Unitatis Redintegratio*, 4.

disappear. Only thus will dialogue help to over-come division and lead us closer to unity.

30. It can be said, with a sense of lively gratitude to the Spirit of Truth, that the Second Vatican Council was a blessed time, during which the bases for the Catholic Church's participation in ecumenical dialogue were laid. At the same time, the presence of many observers from various Churches and Ecclesial Communities, their deep involvement in the events of the Council, the many meetings and the common prayer which the Council made possible, also helped bring about *the conditions for dialogue with one another*. During the Council, the representatives of other Churches and Ecclesial Communities experienced the readiness of the worldwide Catholic Episcopate, and in particular of the Apostolic See, to engage in dialogue.

Local structures of dialogue

31. The Church's commitment to ecumenical dialogue, as it has clearly appeared since the Council, far from being the responsibility of the Apostolic See alone, is also the duty of individual local or particular Churches. Special commissions for fostering the ecumenical spirit and ecumenical activity have been set up by the Bishops' Confer-ences and the Synods of the Eastern Catholic Churches. Suitable structures similar to these are operating in individual Dioceses. These initiatives are a sign of the widespread practical commitment

of the Catholic Church to apply the Council's guidelines on ecumenism: this is an essential aspect of the ecumenical movement.[55] Dialogue has not only been undertaken; it *has become an outright necessity, one of the Church's priorities*. As a result, the "methods" of dialogue have been improved, which in turn has helped the spirit of dialogue to grow. In this context mention has to be made in the first place of "dialogue between competent experts from different Churches and Communities. In their meetings, which are organized in a religious spirit, each explains the teaching of his Communion in greater depth and brings out clearly its distinctive features".[56] Moreover, it is useful for all the faithful to be familiar with the method which makes dialogue possible.

32.   As the Council's Declaration on Religious Freedom affirms: "Truth is to be sought after in a manner proper to the dignity of the human person and his social nature. The inquiry is to be free, carried on with the aid of teaching or instruction, communication, and dialogue. In the course of these, people explain to one another the truth they have discovered, or think they have discovered, in order thus to assist one another in the quest for truth. Moreover, as the truth is discovered, it is by a personal assent that individuals are to adhere to it".[57]

[55] Cf. *Code of Canon Law*, Canon 755; *Code of Canons of the Eastern Churches*, Canons 902-904.
[56] Cf. SECOND VATICAN ECUMENICAL COUNCIL, Decree on Ecumenism *Unitatis Redintegratio*, 4.
[57] SECOND VATICAN ECUMENICAL COUNCIL, Declaration on Religious Freedom *Dignitatis Humanæ*, 3.

Ecumenical dialogue is of essential importance. "Through such dialogue everyone gains a truer knowledge and *more just appreciation* of the teaching and religious life of both Communions. In addition, these Communions *cooperate more closely* in whatever projects a Christian conscience demands for the common good. They also come together for common prayer, where that is permitted. Finally, all are led to examine their own faithfulness to Christ's will for the Church and, wherever necessary, undertake with vigour the tasks of renewal and reform".[58]

Dialogue as an examination of conscience

33.   In the Council's thinking, ecumenical dialogue is marked by a common quest for truth, particularly concerning the Church. In effect, truth forms consciences and directs efforts to promote unity. At the same time, it demands that the consciences and actions of Christians, as brethren divided from one another, should be inspired by and submissive to Christ's prayer for unity. There is a close relationship between prayer and dialogue. Deeper and more conscious prayer makes dialogue more fruitful. If on the one hand, dialogue depends on prayer, so, in another sense, prayer also becomes the ever more mature fruit of dialogue.

34.   Thanks to ecumenical dialogue we can speak of a greater maturity in our common prayer

[58] SECOND VATICAN ECUMENICAL COUNCIL, Decree on Ecumenism *Unitatis Redintegratio*, 4.

for one another. This is possible inasmuch as *dialogue also serves as an examination of conscience*. In this context, how can we fail to recall the words of the First Letter of John? "If we say we have no sin, we deceive ourselves, and the truth is not in us. If we confess our sins, God is faithful and just, and will forgive our sins and cleanse us from all unrighteousness" (1:8-9). John even goes so far as to state: "If we say that we have not sinned, we make him a liar, and his word is not in us" (1:10). *Such a radical exhortation to acknowledge our condition as sinners* ought also to mark the spirit which we bring to ecumenical dialogue. If such dialogue does not become an examination of conscience, a kind of "dialogue of consciences", can we count on the assurance which the First Letter of John gives us? "My little children, I am writing this to you so that you may not sin; but if any one does sin, *we have an advocate with the Father, Jesus Christ the righteous*; and he is the expiation for our sins, and not for ours only but also for the sins of the whole world" (2:1-2). All the sins of the world were gathered up in the saving sacrifice of Christ, including the sins committed against the Church's unity: the sins of Christians, those of the pastors no less than those of the lay faithful. Even after the many sins which have contributed to our historical divisions, *Christian unity is possible*, provided that we are humbly conscious of having sinned against unity and are convinced of our need for conversion. Not only personal sins must be forgiven and left behind, but also social sins, which is to say the sinful "structures" themselves which have contributed and can still contribute to division and to the reinforcing of division.

35.   Here once again the Council proves helpful. It can be said that the entire Decree on Ecumenism is permeated by the spirit of conversion.[59] In the Document, ecumenical dialogue takes on a specific characteristic; it becomes a *"dialogue of conversion"*, and thus, in the words of Pope Paul VI, an authentic "dialogue of salvation".[60] Dialogue cannot take place merely on a horizontal level, being restricted to meetings, exchanges of points of view or even the sharing of gifts proper to each Community. It has also a primarily vertical thrust, directed towards the One who, as the Redeemer of the world and the Lord of history, is himself our Reconciliation. This vertical aspect of dialogue lies in our acknowledgment, jointly and to each other, that we are men and women who have sinned. It is precisely this acknowledgment which creates in brothers and sisters living in Communities not in full communion with one another that interior space where Christ, the source of the Church's unity, can effectively act, with all the power of his Spirit, the Paraclete.

Dialogue as a means of resolving disagreements

36.   Dialogue is also a natural instrument for comparing differing points of view and, above all,

---

[59] Cf. *ibid.*
[60] Encyclical Letter *Ecclesiam Suam* (6 August 1964), III: *AAS* 56 (1964), 642.

for examining those disagreements which hinder full communion between Christians. The Decree on Ecumenism dwells in the first place on a description of the attitudes under which doctrinal discussions should take place: "Catholic theologians engaged in ecumenical dialogue, while standing fast by the teaching of the Church and searching together with separated brothers and sisters into the divine mysteries, should act with love for truth, with charity, and with humility".[61]

Love for the truth is the deepest dimension of any authentic quest for full communion between Christians. Without this love it would be impossible to face the objective theological, cultural, psychological and social difficulties which appear when disagreements are examined. This dimension, which is interior and personal, must be inseparably accompanied by a spirit of charity and humility. There must be charity towards one's partner in dialogue, and humility with regard to the truth which comes to light and which might require a review of assertions and attitudes.

With regard to the study of areas of disagreement, the Council requires that the whole body of doctrine be clearly presented. At the same time, it asks that the manner and method of expounding the Catholic faith should not be a hindrance to dialogue with our brothers and sisters.[62] Certainly it is possible to profess one's faith and to explain its teaching in a way that is correct, fair and under-

[61] SECOND VATICAN ECUMENICAL COUNCIL, Decree on Ecumenism *Unitatis Redintegratio*, 11.
[62] Cf. *ibid.*

standable, and which at the same time takes into account both the way of thinking and the actual historical experiences of the other party.

Full communion of course will have to come about through the acceptance of the whole truth into which the Holy Spirit guides Christ's disciples. Hence all forms of reductionism or facile "agreement" must be absolutely avoided. Serious questions must be resolved, for if not, they will reappear at another time, either in the same terms or in a different guise.

37.   The Decree *Unitatis Redintegratio* also indicates a criterion to be followed when Catholics are presenting or comparing doctrines: "They should remember that in Catholic teaching there exists an order or 'hierarchy' of truths, since they vary in their relationship to the foundation of the Christian faith. Thus the way will be opened for this kind of fraternal rivalry to incite all to a deeper realization and a clearer expression of the unfathomable riches of Christ".[63]

38.   In dialogue, one inevitably comes up against the problem of the different formulations whereby doctrine is expressed in the various Churches and Ecclesial Communities. This has more than one consequence for the work of ecumenism.

In the first place, with regard to doctrinal formulations which differ from those normally in

[63] *Ibid.*; cf. CONGREGATION FOR THE DOCTRINE OF THE FAITH, Declaration in Defence of Catholic Doctrine on the Church *Mysterium Ecclesiæ* (24 June 1973), 4: *AAS* 65 (1973), 402.

use in the community to which one belongs, it is certainly right to determine whether the words involved say the same thing. This has been ascertained in the case for example of the recent common declarations signed by my Predecessors or by myself with the Patriarchs of Churches with which for centuries there have been disputes about Christology. As far as the formulation of revealed truths is concerned, the Declaration *Mysterium Ecclesiae* states: "Even though the truths which the Church intends to teach through her dogmatic formulas are distinct from the changeable conceptions of a given epoch and can be expressed without them, nevertheless it can sometimes happen that these truths may be enunciated by the Sacred Magisterium in terms that bear traces of such conceptions. In view of this, it must be stated that the dogmatic *formulas* of the Church's Magisterium were from the very beginning suitable for communicating revealed truth, and that as they are they remain for ever suitable for communicating this truth to those who interpret them correctly".[64] In this regard, ecumenical dialogue, which prompts the parties involved to question each other, to understand each other and to explain their positions to each other, makes surprising discoveries possible. Intolerant polemics and controversies have made incompatible assertions out of what was really the result of two different ways of looking at the same reality. Nowadays we

---

[64] CONGREGATION FOR THE DOCTRINE OF THE FAITH, Declaration in Defence of Catholic Doctrine on the Church *Mysterium Ecclesiæ*, 5: *AAS* 65 (1973), 403.

need to find the formula which, by capturing the reality in its entirety, will enable us to move beyond partial readings and eliminate false interpretations.

One of the advantages of ecumenism is that it helps Christian Communities to discover the unfathomable riches of the truth. Here too, everything that the Spirit brings about in "others" can serve for the building up of all Communities [65] and in a certain sense instruct them in the mystery of Christ. Authentic ecumenism is a gift at the service of truth.

39. Finally, dialogue puts before the participants real and genuine disagreements in matters of faith. Above all, these disagreements should be faced in a sincere spirit of fraternal charity, of respect for the demands of one's own conscience and of the conscience of the other party, with profound humility and love for the truth. The examination of such disagreements has two essential points of reference: Sacred Scripture and the great Tradition of the Church. Catholics have the help of the Church's living Magisterium.

Practical cooperation

40. Relations between Christians are not aimed merely at mutual knowledge, common prayer and dialogue. They presuppose and from now on call for every possible form of practical cooperation at

[65] Cf. SECOND VATICAN ECUMENICAL COUNCIL, Decree on Ecumenism *Unitatis Redintegratio*, 4.

all levels: pastoral, cultural and social, as well as that of witnessing to the Gospel message.[66]

"Cooperation among all Christians vividly expresses that bond which already unites them, and it sets in clearer relief the features of Christ the Servant".[67] This cooperation based on our common faith is not only filled with fraternal communion, but is a manifestation of Christ himself.

Moreover, ecumenical cooperation is a true school of ecumenism, a dynamic road to unity. Unity of action leads to the full unity of faith: "Through such cooperation, all believers in Christ are able to learn easily how they can understand each other better and esteem each other more, and how the road to the unity of Christians may be made smooth".[68]

In the eyes of the world, cooperation among Christians becomes a form of common Christian witness and a means of evangelization which benefits all involved.

---

[66] Cf. Common Christological Declaration between the Catholic Church and the Assyrian Church of the East: *L'Osservatore Romano,* 12 November 1994, 1.

[67] SECOND VATICAN ECUMENICAL COUNCIL, Decree on Ecumenism *Unitatis Redintegratio,* 12.

[68] *Ibid.*

CHAPTER II

THE FRUITS OF DIALOGUE

Brotherhood rediscovered

41.   What has been said above about ecumenical dialogue since the end of the Council inspires us to give thanks to the Spirit of Truth promised by Christ the Lord to the Apostles and the Church (cf. *Jn* 14:26). It is the first time in history that efforts on behalf of Christian unity have taken on such great proportions and have become so extensive. This is truly an immense gift of God, one which deserves all our gratitude. From the fullness of Christ we receive "grace upon grace" (*Jn* 1:16). An appreciation of how much God has already given is the condition which disposes us to receive those gifts still indispensable for bringing to completion the ecumenical work of unity.

An overall view of the last thirty years enables us better to appreciate many of the fruits of this common conversion to the Gospel which the Spirit of God has brought about by means of the ecumenical movement.

42.   It happens for example that, in the spirit of the Sermon on the Mount, Christians of one confession no longer consider other Christians as en-

emies or strangers but see them as brothers and sisters. Again, the very expression *separated breth-ren* tends to be replaced today by expressions which more readily evoke the deep communion — linked to the baptismal character — which the Spirit fosters in spite of historical and canonical divisions. Today we speak of "other Christians", "others who have received Baptism", and "Christians of other Communities". The *Directory for the Application of Principles and Norms on Ecumenism* refers to the Communities to which these Christians belong as "Churches and Ecclesial Communities that are not in full communion with the Catholic Church".[69] This broadening of vocabulary is indicative of a significant change in attitudes. There is an increased awareness that we all belong to Christ. I have personally been able many times to observe this during the ecumenical celebrations which are an important part of my Apostolic Visits to various parts of the world, and also in the meetings and ecumenical celebrations which have taken place in Rome. The "universal brotherhood" of Christians has become a firm ecumenical conviction. Consigning to oblivion the excommunications of the past, Communities which were once rivals are now in many cases helping one another: places of worship are sometimes lent out; scholarships are offered for the training of ministers in the Communities most lacking in resources; approaches are made to civil authorities on behalf

---

[69] PONTIFICAL COUNCIL FOR PROMOTING CHRISTIAN UNITY, *Directory for the Application of Principles and Norms on Ecumenism* (25 March 1993), 5: *AAS* 85 (1993), 1040.

of other Christians who are unjustly persecuted; and the slander to which certain groups are subjected is shown to be unfounded.

In a word, Christians have been converted to a fraternal charity which embraces all Christ's disciples. If it happens that, as a result of violent political disturbances, a certain aggressiveness or a spirit of vengeance appears, the leaders of the parties in question generally work to make the "New Law" of the spirit of charity prevail. Unfortunately, this spirit has not been able to transform every situation where brutal conflict rages. In such circumstances those committed to ecumenism are often required to make choices which are truly heroic.

It needs be reaffirmed in this regard that acknowledging our brotherhood is not the consequence of a large-hearted philanthropy or a vague family spirit. It is rooted in recognition of the oneness of Baptism and the subsequent duty to glorify God in his work. The *Directory for the Application of Principles and Norms on Ecumenism* expresses the hope that Baptisms will be mutually and officially recognized.[70] This is something much more than an act of ecumenical courtesy; it constitutes a basic ecclesiological statement.

It is fitting to recall that the fundamental role of Baptism in building up the Church has been clearly brought out thanks also to multilateral dialogues.[71]

---

[70] *Ibid.* 94: *loc. cit.*, 1078.
[71] Cf. COMMISSION ON FAITH AND ORDER OF THE WORLD COUNCIL OF CHURCHES, *Baptism, Eucharist and Ministry* (January 1982).

43.   It happens more and more often that the leaders of Christian Communities join together in taking a stand in the name of Christ on important problems concerning man's calling and on freedom, justice, peace, and the future of the world. In this way they "communicate" in one of the tasks which constitutes the mission of Christians: that of reminding society of God's will in a realistic manner, warning the authorities and their fellow-citizens against taking steps which would lead to the trampling of human rights. It is clear, as experience shows, that in some circumstances the united voice of Christians has more impact than any one isolated voice.

Nor are the leaders of Communities the only ones joined in the work for unity. Many Christians from all Communities, by reason of their faith, are jointly involved in bold projects aimed at changing the world by inculcating respect for the rights and needs of everyone, especially the poor, the lowly and the defenceless. In my Encyclical Letter *Sollicitudo Rei Socialis*, I was pleased to note this cooperation, stressing that the Catholic Church cannot fail to take part in these efforts.[72] In effect, Christians who once acted independently are now engaged together in the service of this cause, so that God's mercy may triumph.

This way of thinking and acting is already that of the Gospel. Hence, reaffirming what I wrote in

---

[72] Cf. Encyclical Letter *Sollicitudo Rei Socialis* (30 December 1987), 32: *AAS* 80 (1988), 556.

my first Encyclical Letter *Redemptor Hominis*, I have had occasion "to insist on this point and to encourage every effort made in this direction, at all levels where we meet our other brother Christians".[73] I have thanked God "for what he has already accomplished in the other Churches and Ecclesial Communities and through them", as well as through the Catholic Church.[74] Today I see with satisfaction that the already vast network of ecumenical cooperation is constantly growing. Thanks also to the influence of the World Council of Churches, much is being accomplished in this field.

Approaching one another through the Word of God and through divine worship

44.   Significant progress in ecumenical cooperation has also been made in another area, that of the Word of God. I am thinking above all of the importance for the different language groups of ecumenical translations of the Bible. Following the promulgation by the Second Vatican Council of the Constitution *Dei Verbum*, the Catholic Church could not fail to welcome this development.[75] These

[73] Address to the Cardinals and the Roman Curia (28 June 1985), 10: *AAS* 77 (1985), 1158; cf. Encyclical Letter *Redemptor Hominis* (4 March 1979), 11: *AAS* 71 (1979), 277-278.

[74] Address to the Cardinals and the Roman Curia (28 June 1985), 10: *AAS* 77 (1985), 1158.

[75] Cf. SECRETARIAT FOR PROMOTING CHRISTIAN UNITY and the EXECUTIVE COMMITTEE OF THE UNITED BIBLE SOCIETIES, *Guiding Principles for Interconfessional Cooperation in Translating the Bible* (1968). This was revised and then published by the SECRETARIAT FOR PROMOTING CHRISTIAN UNITY, "Guidelines for

translations, prepared by experts, generally offer a solid basis for the prayer and pastoral activity of all Christ's followers. Anyone who recalls how heavily debates about Scripture influenced divisions, especially in the West, can appreciate the significant step forward which these common translations represent.

45.   Corresponding to the liturgical renewal carried out by the Catholic Church, certain other Ecclesial Communities have made efforts to renew their worship. Some, on the basis of a recommendation expressed at the ecumenical level,[76] have abandoned the custom of celebrating their liturgy of the Lord's Supper only infrequently and have opted for a celebration each Sunday. Again, when the cycles of liturgical readings used by the various Christian Communities in the West are compared, they appear to be essentially the same. Still on the ecumenical level,[77] very special prominence has been given to the liturgy and liturgical signs (images, icons, vestments, light, incense, gestures). Moreover, in schools of theology where future ministers are trained, courses in the history and significance of the liturgy are beginning to be part of the curriculum in response to a newly discovered need.

Interconfessional Cooperation in Translating the Bible": *Information Service,* 65 (1987), 140-145.
     [76] Cf. COMMISSION ON FAITH AND ORDER OF THE WORLD COUNCIL OF CHURCHES, *Baptism, Eucharist and Ministry* (January 1982).
     [77] For example, at the most recent assemblies of the World Council of Churches in Vancouver (1983) and in Canberra (1991), and of the Commission on Faith and Order in Santiago de Compostela (1993).

These are signs of convergence which regard various aspects of the sacramental life. Certainly, due to disagreements in matters of faith, it is not yet possible to celebrate together the same Eucharistic Liturgy. And yet we do have a burning desire to join in celebrating the one Eucharist of the Lord, and this desire itself is already a common prayer of praise, a single supplication. Together we speak to the Father and increasingly we do so "with one heart". At times it seems that we are closer to being able finally to seal this "real although not yet full" communion. A century ago who could even have imagined such a thing?

46.   In this context, it is a source of joy to note that Catholic ministers are able, in certain particular cases, to administer the Sacraments of the Eucharist, Penance and Anointing of the Sick to Christians who are not in full communion with the Catholic Church but who greatly desire to receive these sacraments, freely request them and manifest the faith which the Catholic Church professes with regard to these sacraments. Conversely, in specific cases and in particular circumstances, Catholics too can request these same sacraments from ministers of Churches in which these sacraments are valid. The conditions for such reciprocal reception have been laid down in specific norms; for the sake of furthering ecumenism these norms must be respected.[78]

---

[78] Cf. SECOND VATICAN ECUMENICAL COUNCIL, Decree on Ecumenism *Unitatis Redintegratio,* 8 and 15; *Code of Canon Law,* Canon 844; *Code of Canons of the Eastern Churches,* Canon 671; PONTIFICAL

Appreciating the endowments present among other Christians

47.   Dialogue does not extend exclusively to matters of doctrine but engages the whole person; it is also a dialogue of love. The Council has stated: "Catholics must joyfully acknowledge and esteem the truly Christian endowments from our common heritage which are to be found among our separated brothers and sisters. It is right and salutary to recognize the riches of Christ and virtuous works in the lives of others who are bearing witness to Christ, sometimes even to the shedding of their blood. For God is always wonderful in his works and worthy of admiration".[79]

48.   The relationships which the members of the Catholic Church have established with other Christians since the Council have enabled us to discover what God is bringing about in the members of other Churches and Ecclesial Communities. This direct contact, at a variety of levels, with pastors and with the members of these Communities has made us aware of the witness which other Christians bear to God and to Christ. A vast new field has thus opened up for the whole ecumenical experience, which at the same time is the great challenge of our time. Is not the twentieth century

COUNCIL FOR PROMOTING CHRISTIAN UNITY, *Directory for the Application of Principles and Norms on Ecumenism* (25 March 1993), 122-125, 129-131, 123 and 132: *AAS* 85 (1993), 1086-1087, 1088-1089, 1087 and 1089.
    [79] SECOND VATICAN ECUMENICAL COUNCIL, Decree on Ecumenism *Unitatis Redintegratio*, 4.

a time of great witness, which extends "even to the shedding of blood"? And does not this witness also involve the various Churches and Ecclesial Communities which take their name from Christ, Crucified and Risen?

Such a joint witness of holiness, as fidelity to the one Lord, has an ecumenical potential extraordinarily rich in grace. The Second Vatican Council made it clear that elements present among other Christians can contribute to the edification of Catholics: "Nor should we forget that whatever is wrought by the grace of the Holy Spirit in the hearts of our separated brothers and sisters can contribute to our own edification. Whatever is truly Christian never conflicts with the genuine interests of the faith; indeed, it can always result in a more ample realization of the very mystery of Christ and the Church".[80] Ecumenical dialogue, as a true dialogue of salvation, will certainly encourage this process, which has already begun well, to advance towards true and full communion.

The growth of communion

49.   A valuable result of the contacts between Christians and of the theological dialogue in which they engage is the growth of communion. Both contacts and dialogue have made Christians aware of the elements of faith which they have in common. This has served to consolidate further their commitment to full unity. In all of this,

[80] *Ibid.*

the Second Vatican Council remains a powerful source of incentive and orientation.

The Dogmatic Constitution *Lumen Gentium* links its teaching on the Catholic Church to an acknowledgment of the saving elements found in other Churches and Ecclesial Communities.[81] It is not a matter of becoming aware of static elements passively present in those Churches and Communities. Insofar as they are elements of the Church of Christ, these are by their nature a force for the re-establishment of unity. Consequently, the quest for Christian unity is not a matter of choice or expediency, but a duty which springs from the very nature of the Christian community.

In a similar way, the bilateral theological dialogues carried on with the major Christian Communities start from a recognition of the degree of communion already present, in order to go on to discuss specific areas of disagreement. The Lord has made it possible for Christians in our day to reduce the number of matters traditionally in dispute.

Dialogue with the Churches of the East

50.   In this regard, it must first be acknowledged, with particular gratitude to Divine Providence, that our bonds with the Churches of the East, weakened in the course of the centuries, were strengthened through the Second Vatican Council. The observers from these Churches pres-

[81] Cf. No. 15.

ent at the Council, together with representatives of the Churches and Ecclesial Communities of the West, stated publicly, at that very solemn moment for the Catholic Church, their common willingness to seek the re-establishment of communion.

The Council, for its part, considered the Churches of the East with objectivity and deep affection, stressing their ecclesial nature and the real bonds of communion linking them with the Catholic Church. The Decree on Ecumenism points out: "Through the celebration of the Eucharist of the Lord in each of these Churches, the Church of God is built up and grows in stature". It adds, as a consequence, that "although these Churches are separated from us, they possess true sacraments, above all—by apostolic succession—the priesthood and the Eucharist, whereby they are still joined to us in a very close relationship".[82]

Speaking of the Churches of the East, the Council acknowledged their great liturgical and spiritual tradition, the specific nature of their historical development, the disciplines coming from the earliest times and approved by the Holy Fathers and Ecumenical Councils, and their own particular way of expressing their teaching. The Council made this acknowledgement in the conviction that legitimate diversity is in no way opposed to the Church's unity, but rather enhances her splendour and contributes greatly to the fulfilment of her mission.

[82] No. 15.

The Second Vatican Ecumenical Council wished to base dialogue on the communion which already exists, and it draws attention to the noble reality of the Churches of the East: "Therefore, this Sacred Synod urges all, but especially those who plan to devote themselves to the work of restoring the full communion that is desired between the Eastern Churches and the Catholic Church, to give due consideration to these special aspects of the origin and growth of the Churches of the East, and to the character of the relations which obtained between them and the Roman See before the separation, and to form for themselves a correct evaluation of these facts".[83]

51.   The Council's approach has proved fruitful both for the steady maturing of fraternal relations through the dialogue of charity, and for doctrinal discussion in the framework of the *Joint International Commission for the Theological Dialogue between the Catholic Church and the Orthodox Church*. It has likewise proved most fruitful in relations with the Ancient Churches of the East.

The process has been slow and arduous, yet a source of great joy; and it has been inspiring, for it has led to the gradual rediscovery of brotherhood.

Resuming contacts

52.   With regard to the Church of Rome and the Ecumenical Patriarchate of Constantinople,

[83] *Ibid.*, 14.

the process which we have just mentioned began thanks to the mutual openness demonstrated by Popes John XXIII and Paul VI on the one hand, and by the Ecumenical Patriarch Athenagoras I and his successors on the other. The resulting change found its historical expression in the ecclesial act whereby "there was removed from memory and from the midst of the Church" [84] the remembrance of the excommunications which nine hundred years before, in 1054, had become the symbol of the schism between Rome and Constantinople. That ecclesial event, so filled with ecumenical commitment, took place during the last days of the Council, on 7 December 1965. The Council thus ended with a solemn act which was at once a healing of historical memories, a mutual forgiveness, and a firm commitment to strive for communion.

This gesture had been preceded by the meeting of Pope Paul VI and Patriarch Athenagoras I in Jerusalem, in January 1964, during the Pope's pilgrimage to the Holy Land. At that time Pope Paul was also able to meet Benedictos, the Orthodox Patriarch of Jerusalem. Later, Pope Paul visited Patriarch Athenagoras at the Phanar (Istanbul), on 25 July 1967, and in October of the same year the Patriarch was solemnly received in Rome. These prayer-filled meetings mapped out the path of rapprochement between the Church of the East and the Church of the West, and of the

---

[84] Cf. Joint Declaration of Pope Paul VI and the Patriarch of Constantinople Athenagoras I (7 December 1965): *Tomos Agapis*, Vatican-Phanar (1958-1970), Rome-Istanbul, 1971, 280-281.

re-establishment of the unity they shared in the first millennium.

Following the death of Pope Paul VI and the brief pontificate of Pope John I, when the ministry of Bishop of Rome was entrusted to me, I considered it one of the first duties of my pontificate to renew personal contact with the Ecumenical Patriarch Dimitrios I, who had meanwhile succeeded Patriarch Athenagoras in the See of Constantinople. During my visit to the Phanar on 29 November 1979, the Patriarch and I were able to decide to begin theological dialogue between the Catholic Church and all the Orthodox Churches in canonical communion with the See of Constantinople. In this regard it would seem important to add that at that time preparations were already under way for the convocation of a future Council of the Orthodox Churches. The quest for harmony between them contributes to the life and vitality of these sister Churches; this is also significant in view of the role they are called to play in the path towards unity. The Ecumenical Patriarch decided to repay my visit, and in December 1987 I had the joy of welcoming him to Rome with deep affection and with the solemnity due to him. It is in this context of ecclesial fraternity that we should mention the practice, which has now been in place for a number of years, of welcoming a delegation from the Ecumenical Patriarchate to Rome for the Feast of the Holy Apostles Peter and Paul, as well as the custom of sending a delegation of the Holy See to the Phanar for the solemn celebration of Saint Andrew.

53.   Among other things, these regular contacts permit a direct exchange of information and opinions with a view to fostering fraternal coordination. Furthermore, taking part together in prayer accustoms us once more to living side by side and helps us in accepting and putting into practice the Lord's will for his Church.

On the path which we have travelled since the Second Vatican Council, at least two particularly telling events of great ecumenical significance for relations between East and West should be mentioned. The first of these was the 1984 Jubilee in commemoration of the eleventh centenary of the evangelizing activity of Saints Cyril and Methodius, an occasion which enabled me to proclaim the two Holy Apostles of the Slavs, those heralds of faith, co-patrons of Europe. In 1964, during the Council, Pope Paul VI had already proclaimed Saint Benedict patron of Europe. Associating the two Brothers from Thessalonica with the great founder of Western monasticism serves indirectly to highlight that twofold ecclesial and cultural tradition which has proved so significant for the two thousand years of Christianity which mark the history of Europe. Consequently it is worth recalling that Saints Cyril and Methodius came from the background of the Byzantine Church of their day, at a time when the latter was in communion with Rome. In proclaiming them patrons of Europe, together with Saint Benedict, it was my intention not only to reaffirm the historical truth about Christianity in Europe, but also to provide an important topic for the dialogue between East and West which has raised such high hopes in the period since the Council. As in Saint Benedict, so in Saints Cyril and Methodius, Europe can rediscover its spiritual roots. Now, as the second millennium since the Birth of Christ draws to a close, they must be venerated *together*, as the patrons of our past and as the Saints to whom the Churches and nations of Europe entrust their future.

54.   The other event which I am pleased to recall is the celebration of the Millennium of the Baptism of Rus' (988-1988). The Catholic Church, and this Apostolic See in particular, desired to take part in the Jubilee celebrations and also sought to emphasize that the Baptism conferred on Saint Vladimir in Kiev was a key event in the evangelization of the world. The great Slav nations of Eastern Europe owe their faith to this event, as do the peoples living beyond the Ural Mountains and as far as Alaska.

In this perspective an expression which I have frequently employed finds its deepest meaning: the Church must breathe with her two lungs! In the first millennium of the history of Christianity, this expression refers primarily to the relationship between Byzantium and Rome. From the time of the Baptism of Rus' it comes to have an even wider application: evangelization spread to a much vaster area, so that it now includes the entire Church. If we then consider that the salvific event which took place on the banks of the Dnieper goes back to a time when the Church in the

East and the Church in the West were not divided, we understand clearly that the vision of the full communion to be sought is that of unity in legitimate diversity. This is what I strongly asserted in my Encyclical Epistle *Slavorum Apostoli* [85] on Saints Cyril and Methodius and in my Apostolic Letter *Euntes in Mundum* [86] addressed to the faithful of the Catholic Church in commemoration of the Millennium of the Baptism of Kievan Rus'.

Sister Churches

55.   In its historical survey the Council Decree *Unitatis Redintegratio* has in mind the unity which, in spite of everything, was experienced in the first millennium and in a certain sense now serves as a kind of model. "This most sacred Synod gladly reminds all ... that in the East there flourish many particular or local Churches; among them the Patriarchal Churches hold first place; and of these, many glory in taking their origin from the Apostles themselves".[87] The Church's journey began in Jerusalem on the day of Pentecost and its original expansion in the *oikoumene* of that time was centred around Peter and the Eleven (cf. *Acts* 2:14). The structures of the Church in the East and in the West evolved in reference to that Apostolic heritage. Her unity during the first millenni-

[85] Cf. *AAS* 77 (1985), 779-813.
[86] Cf. *AAS* 80 (1988), 933-956; cf. Message *Magnum Baptismi Donum,* (14 February 1988): *AAS* 80 (1988), 988-997.
[87] SECOND VATICAN ECUMENICAL COUNCIL, Decree on Ecumenism *Unitatis Redintegratio,* 14.

um was maintained within those same structures through the Bishops, Successors of the Apostles, in communion with the Bishop of Rome. If today at the end of the second millennium we are seeking to restore full communion, it is to that unity, thus structured, which we must look.

The Decree on Ecumenism highlights a further distinctive aspect, thanks to which all the particular Churches remained in unity: "an eager desire to perpetuate in a communion of faith and charity those family ties which ought to thrive between local Churches, as between sisters".[88]

56. Following the Second Vatican Council, and in the light of earlier tradition, it has again become usual to refer to the particular or local Churches gathered around their Bishop as "Sister Churches". In addition, the lifting of the mutual excommunications, by eliminating a painful canonical and psychological obstacle, was a very significant step on the way towards full communion.

The structures of unity which existed before the separation are a heritage of experience that guides our common path towards the re-establishment of full communion. Obviously, during the second millennium the Lord has not ceased to bestow on his Church abundant fruits of grace and growth. Unfortunately, however, the gradual and mutual estrangement between the Churches of the West and the East deprived them of the benefits

[88] *Ibid.*

of mutual exchanges and cooperation. With the grace of God a great effort must be made to re-establish full communion among them, the source of such good for the Church of Christ. This effort calls for all our good will, humble prayer and a steadfast cooperation which never yields to discouragement. Saint Paul urges us: "Bear one another's burdens" (*Gal* 6:2). How appropriate and relevant for us is the Apostle's exhortation! The traditional designation of "Sister Churches" should ever accompany us along this path.

57.   In accordance with the hope expressed by Pope Paul VI, our declared purpose is to re-establish together full unity in legitimate diversity: "God has granted us to receive in faith what the Apostles saw, understood, and proclaimed to us. By Baptism 'we are *one in Christ Jesus*' (*Gal* 3:28). In virtue of the apostolic succession, we are united more closely by the priesthood and the Eucharist. By participating in the gifts of God to his Church we are brought into communion with the Father through the Son in the Holy Spirit ... In each local Church this mystery of divine love is enacted, and surely this is the ground of the traditional and very beautiful expression 'Sister Churches', which local Churches were fond of applying to one another (cf. Decree, *Unitatis Redintegratio*, 14). For centuries we lived this life of 'Sister Churches', and together held Ecumenical Councils which guarded the deposit of faith against all corruption. And now, after a long period of division and

mutual misunderstanding, the Lord is enabling us to discover ourselves as 'Sister Churches' once more, in spite of the obstacles which were once raised between us".[89] If today, on the threshold of the third millennium, we are seeking the re-establishment of full communion, it is for the accomplishment of this reality that we must work and it is to this reality that we must refer.

Contact with this glorious tradition is most fruitful for the Church. As the Council points out: "From their very origins the Churches of the East have had a treasury from which the Church of the West has amply drawn for its liturgy, spiritual tradition and jurisprudence".[90]

Part of this "treasury" are also "the riches of those spiritual traditions to which monasticism gives special expression. From the glorious days of the Holy Fathers, there flourished in the East that monastic spirituality which later flowed over into the Western world".[91] As I have had the occasion to emphasize in my recent Apostolic Letter *Orientale Lumen*, the Churches of the East have lived with great generosity the commitment shown by monastic life, "starting with evangelization, the highest service that the Christian can offer his brother, followed by many other forms of spiritual and material service. Indeed it can be said that monasticism in antiquity—and at various times in

[89] Apostolic Brief *Anno Ineunte* (25 July 1967): *Tomos Agapis*, Vatican-Phanar (1958-1970), Rome-Istanbul, 1971, 388-391.
[90] SECOND VATICAN ECUMENICAL COUNCIL, Decree on Ecumenism *Unitatis Redintegratio*, 14.
[91] *Ibid.*, 15.

subsequent ages too—has been the privileged means for the evangelization of peoples".[92]

The Council does not limit itself to emphasizing the elements of similarity between the Churches in the East and in the West. In accord with historical truth, it does not hesitate to say: "It is hardly surprising if sometimes one tradition has come nearer than the other to an apt appreciation of certain aspects of the revealed mystery or has expressed them in a clearer manner. As a result, these various theological formulations are often to be considered as complementary rather than conflicting".[93] Communion is made fruitful by the exchange of gifts between the Churches insofar as they complement each other.

58.   From the reaffirmation of an already existing communion of faith, the Second Vatican Council drew pastoral consequences which are useful for the everyday life of the faithful and for the promotion of the spirit of unity. By reason of the very close sacramental bonds between the Catholic Church and the Orthodox Churches, the Decree on Eastern Catholic Churches *Orientalium Ecclesiarum* has stated: "Pastoral experience clearly shows that with respect to our Eastern brethren there should and can be taken into consideration various circumstances affecting individuals, wherein the unity of the Church is not jeopardized nor are intolerable risks involved, but

[92] No. 14: *L'Osservatore Romano*, 2-3 May 1995, 3.
[93] SECOND VATICAN ECUMENICAL COUNCIL, Decree on Ecumenism *Unitatis Redintegratio*, 17.

in which salvation itself and the spiritual profit of souls are urgently at issue. Hence, in view of special circumstances of time, place and personage, the Catholic Church has often adopted and now adopts a milder policy, offering to all the means of salvation and an example of charity among Christians through participation in the Sacraments and in other sacred functions and objects".[94]

In the light of experience gained in the years following the Council, this theological and pastoral orientation has been incorporated into the two Codes of Canon Law.[95] It has been explicitly treated from the pastoral standpoint in the *Directory for the Application of Principles and Norms on Ecumenism*.[96]

In so important and sensitive a matter, it is necessary for Pastors to instruct the faithful with care, making them clearly aware of the specific reasons both for this sharing in liturgical worship and for the various regulations which govern it.

There must never be a loss of appreciation for the ecclesiological implication of sharing in the sacraments, especially in the Holy Eucharist.

---

[94] No. 26.

[95] Cf. *Code of Canon Law*, Canon 844, §§ 2 and 3; *Code of Canons of the Eastern Churches*, Canon 671, §§ 2 and 3.

[96] PONTIFICAL COUNCIL FOR PROMOTING CHRISTIAN UNITY, *Directory for the Application of Principles and Norms on Ecumenism* (25 March 1993), 122-128: *AAS* 85 (1993), 1086-1088.

59.   Since its establishment in 1979, the *Joint International Commission for the Theological Dialogue between the Catholic Church and the Orthodox Church* has worked steadily, directing its study to areas decided upon by mutual agreement, with the purpose of re-establishing full communion between the two Churches. This communion which is founded on the unity of faith, following in the footsteps of the experience and tradition of the ancient Church, will find its fulfilment in the common celebration of the Holy Eucharist. In a positive spirit, and on the basis of what we have in common, the Joint Commission has been able to make substantial progress and, as I was able to declare in union with my Venerable Brother, His Holiness Dimitrios I, the Ecumenical Patriarch, it has concluded "that the Catholic Church and the Orthodox Church can already profess together that common faith in the mystery of the Church and the bond between faith and sacraments".[97] The Commission was then able to acknowledge that "in our Churches apostolic succession is fundamental for the sanctification and the unity of the people of God".[98] These are important points of

---

[97] Declaration by His Holiness Pope John Paul II and the Ecumenical Patriarch Dimitrios I (7 December 1987): *AAS* 80 (1988), 253.

[98] JOINT INTERNATIONAL COMMISSION FOR THE THEOLOGICAL DIALOGUE BETWEEN THE CATHOLIC CHURCH AND THE ORTHODOX CHURCH, "The Sacrament of Order in the Sacramental Structure of the Church, with Particular Reference to the Importance of the Apostolic Succession for the Sanctification and the Unity of the People of God" (26 June 1988), 1: *Information Service*, 68 (1988), 173.

reference for the continuation of the dialogue. Moreover, these joint affirmations represent the basis for Catholics and Orthodox to be able from now on to bear a faithful and united common witness in our time, that the name of the Lord may be proclaimed and glorified.

60.   More recently, the Joint International Commission took a significant step forward with regard to the very sensitive question of the method to be followed in re-establishing full communion between the Catholic Church and the Orthodox Church, an issue which has frequently embittered relations between Catholics and Orthodox. The Commission has laid the doctrinal foundations for a positive solution to this problem on the basis of the doctrine of Sister Churches. Here too it has become evident that the method to be followed towards full communion is the dialogue of truth, fostered and sustained by the dialogue of love. A recognition of the right of the Eastern Catholic Churches to have their own organizational structures and to carry out their own apostolate, as well as the actual involvement of these Churches in the dialogue of charity and in theological dialogue, will not only promote a true and fraternal mutual esteem between Orthodox and Catholics living in the same territory, but will also foster their joint commitment to work for unity.[99] A step forward has been taken. The com-

---

[99] Cf. JOHN PAUL II, Letter to the Bishops of Europe on the Relations between Catholics and Orthodox in the New Situation of Central and Eastern Europe (31 May 1991), 6: AAS 84 (1992), 168.

mitment must continue. Already there are signs of a lessening of tensions, which is making the quest for unity more fruitful.

With regard to the Eastern Catholic Churches in communion with the Catholic Church, the Council expressed its esteem in these terms: "While thanking God that many Eastern sons of the Catholic Church ... are already living in full communion with their brethren who follow the tradition of the West, this sacred Synod declares that this entire heritage of spirituality and liturgy, of discipline and theology, in their various traditions, belongs to the full catholic and apostolic character of the Church".[100] Certainly the Eastern Catholic Churches, in the spirit of the Decree on Ecumenism, will play a constructive role in the dialogue of love and in the theological dialogue at both the local and international levels, and thus contribute to mutual understanding and the continuing pursuit of full unity.[101]

61.   In view of all this, the Catholic Church desires nothing less than full communion between East and West. She finds inspiration for this in the experience of the first millennium. In that period, indeed, "the development of different experiences of ecclesial life did not prevent Christians, through mutual relations, from continuing to feel certain that they were at home in any

[100] SECOND VATICAN ECUMENICAL COUNCIL, Decree on Ecumenism *Unitatis Redintegratio*, 17.
[101] Cf. Apostolic Letter *Orientale Lumen* (2 May 1995), 24: *L'Osservatore Romano*, 2-3 May 1995, 5.

Church, because praise of the one Father, through Christ in the Holy Spirit, rose from them all, in a marvellous variety of languages and melodies; all were gathered together to celebrate the Eucharist, the heart and model for the community regarding not only spirituality and the moral life, but also the Church's very structure, in the variety of ministries and services under the leadership of the Bishop, successor of the Apostles. The first Councils are an eloquent witness to this enduring unity in diversity".[102] How can unity be restored after almost a thousand years? This is the great task which the Catholic Church must accomplish, a task equally incumbent on the Orthodox Church. Thus can be understood the continuing relevance of dialogue, guided by the light and strength of the Holy Spirit.

Relations with the Ancient Churches of the East

62. In the period following the Second Vatican Council, the Catholic Church has also, in different ways and with greater or lesser rapidity, restored fraternal relations with the Ancient Churches of the East which rejected the dogmatic formulations of the Councils of Ephesus and Chalcedon. All these Churches sent official observers to the Second Vatican Council; their Patriarchs have honoured us by their visits, and the Bishop of Rome has been able to converse with them as with brothers who, after a long time, joyfully meet again.

[102] *Ibid.*, 18: *loc. cit.*, 4.

The return of fraternal relations with the Ancient Churches of the East witnesses to the Christian faith in situations which are often hostile and tragic. This is a concrete sign of how we are united in Christ in spite of historical, political, social and cultural barriers. And precisely in relation to Christology, we have been able to join the Patriarchs of some of these Churches in declaring our common faith in Jesus Christ, true God and true man. Pope Paul VI of venerable memory signed declarations to this effect with His Holiness Shenouda III, the Coptic Orthodox Pope and Patriarch,[103] and with His Beatitude Jacoub III, the Syrian Orthodox Patriarch of Antioch.[104] I myself have been able to confirm this Christological agreement and draw on it for the development of dialogue with Pope Shenouda,[105] and for pastoral cooperation with the Syrian Patriarch of Antioch Mor Ignatius Zakka I Iwas.[106]

When the Venerable Patriarch of the Ethiopian Church, Abuna Paulos, paid me a visit in Rome on 11 June 1993, together we emphasized the deep communion existing between our two Churches: "We share the faith handed down from

[103] Cf. Joint Declaration by His Holiness Pope Paul VI and His Holiness Shenouda III, Pope of Alexandria and Patriarch of the See of Saint Mark of Alexandria (10 May 1973): *AAS* 65 (1973), 299-301.

[104] Cf. Joint Declaration by His Holiness Pope Paul VI and His Beatitude Mar Ignatius Jacoub III, Patriarch of the Church of Antioch of the Syrians (27 October 1971): *AAS* 63 (1971), 814-815.

[105] Cf. Address to the Delegates of the Coptic Orthodox Church (2 June 1979): *AAS* 71 (1979), 1000-1001.

[106] Cf. Joint Declaration of Pope John Paul II and the Syrian-Orthodox Patriarch of Antioch, Moran Mor Ignatius Zakka I Iwas (23 June 1984): *Insegnamenti* VII/1 (1984), 1902-1906.

the Apostles, as also the same sacraments and the same ministry, rooted in the apostolic succession ... Today, moreover, we can affirm that we have the one faith in Christ, even though for a long time this was a source of division between us".[107]

More recently, the Lord has granted me the great joy of signing a common Christological declaration with the Assyrian Patriarch of the East, His Holiness Mar Dinkha IV, who for this purpose chose to visit me in Rome in November 1994. Taking into account the different theological formulations, we were able to profess together the true faith in Christ.[108] I wish to express my joy at all this in the words of the Blessed Virgin: "My soul proclaims the greatness of the Lord" (*Lk* 1:46).

63.   Ecumenical contacts have thus made possible essential clarifications with regard to the traditional controversies concerning Christology, so much so that we have been able to profess together the faith which we have in common. Once again it must be said that this important achievement is truly a fruit of theological investigation and fraternal dialogue. And not only this. It is an encouragement for us: for it shows us that the path followed is the right one and that we can reasonably hope to discover together the solution to other disputed questions.

---

[107] Address to His Holiness Abuna Paulos, Patriarch of the Orthodox Church of Ethiopia (11 June 1993): *L'Osservatore Romano*, 11-12 June 1993, 4.
[108] Cf. Common Christological Declaration between the Catholic Church and the Assyrian Church of the East: *L'Osservatore Romano*, 12 November 1994, 1.

Dialogue with other Churches and Ecclesial Communities in the West

64.   In its great plan for the re-establishment of unity among all Christians, the Decree on Ecumenism also speaks of relations with the Churches and Ecclesial Communities of the West. Wishing to create a climate of Christian fraternity and dialogue, the Council situates its guidelines in the context of two general considerations: one of an historical and psychological nature, and the other theological and doctrinal. On the one hand, this Decree affirms: "The Churches and Ecclesial Communities which were separated from the Apostolic See of Rome during the very serious crisis that began in the West at the end of the Middle Ages, or during later times, are bound to the Catholic Church by a special affinity and close relationship in view of the long span of earlier centuries when the Christian people lived in ecclesiastical communion".[109] On the other hand, with equal realism the same Document states: "At the same time one should recognize that between these Churches and Communities on the one hand, and the Catholic Church on the other, there are very weighty differences not only of a historical, sociological, psychological and cultural nature, but especially in the interpretation of revealed truth".[110]

---

[109] SECOND VATICAN ECUMENICAL COUNCIL, Decree on Ecumenism *Unitatis Redintegratio*, 19.
[110] *Ibid*.

65.   Common roots and similar, if distinct, considerations have guided the development in the West of the Catholic Church and of the Churches and Communities which have their origins in the Reformation. Consequently these share the fact that they are "Western" in character. Their "diversities", although significant as has been pointed out, do not therefore preclude mutual interaction and complementarity.

The ecumenical movement really began within the Churches and Ecclesial Communities of the Reform. At about the same time, in January, 1920, the Ecumenical Patriarchate expressed the hope that some kind of cooperation among the Christian Communions could be organized. This fact shows that the weight of cultural background is not the decisive factor. What is essential is the question of faith. The prayer of Christ, our one Lord, Redeemer and Master, speaks to everyone in the same way, both in the East and in the West. That prayer becomes an imperative to leave behind our divisions in order to seek and re-establish unity, as a result also of the bitter experiences of division itself.

66.   The Second Vatican Council did not attempt to give a "description" of post-Reformation Christianity, since "in origin, teaching and spiritual practice, these Churches and Ecclesial Communities differ not only from us but also among themselves to a considerable degree".[111] Further-

[111] *Ibid.*, 19.

more, the Decree observes that the ecumenical movement and the desire for peace with the Catholic Church have not yet taken root everywhere.[112] These circumstances notwithstanding, the Council calls for dialogue.

The Council Decree then seeks to "propose ... some considerations which can and ought to serve as a basis and motivation for such dialogue".[113]

"Our thoughts are concerned ... with those Christians who openly confess Jesus Christ as God and Lord and as the sole Mediator between God and man unto the glory of the one God, Father, Son and Holy Spirit".[114]

These brothers and sisters promote love and veneration for the Sacred Scriptures: "Calling upon the Holy Spirit, they seek in these Sacred Scriptures God as he speaks to them in Christ, the One whom the prophets foretold, God's Word made flesh for us. In the Scriptures they contemplate the life of Christ, as well as the teachings and the actions of the Divine Master on behalf of the salvation of all, in particular the mysteries of his Death and Resurrection ... They affirm the divine authority of the Sacred Books".[115]

At the same time, however, they "think differently from us ... about the relationship between the Scriptures and the Church. In the Church, according to Catholic belief, an authentic teaching office plays a special role in the explanation and

[112] Cf. *ibid.*
[113] *Ibid.*
[114] *Ibid.*, 20.
[115] *Ibid.*, 21.

proclamation of the written word of God".[116] Even so, "in [ecumenical] dialogue itself, the sacred utterances are precious instruments in the mighty hand of God for attaining that unity which the Saviour holds out to all".[117]

Furthermore, the Sacrament of Baptism, which we have in common, represents "a sacramental bond of unity linking all who have been reborn by means of it".[118] The theological, pastoral and ecumenical implications of our common Baptism are many and important. Although this sacrament of itself is "only a beginning, a point of departure", it is "oriented towards a complete profession of faith, a complete incorporation into the system of salvation such as Christ himself willed it to be, and finally, towards a complete participation in Eucharistic communion".[119]

67.   Doctrinal and historical disagreements at the time of the Reformation emerged with regard to the Church, the sacraments and the ordained ministry. The Council therefore calls for "dialogue to be undertaken concerning the true meaning of the Lord's Supper, the other sacraments and the Church's worship and ministry".[120]

The Decree *Unitatis Redintegratio*, pointing out that the post-Reformation Communities lack that "fullness of unity with us which should flow from Baptism", observes that "especially because

[116] *Ibid.*
[117] *Ibid.*
[118] *Ibid.*, 22.
[119] *Ibid.*
[120] *Ibid.*, 22; cf. 20.

78

of the lack of the Sacrament of Orders they have not preserved the genuine and total reality of the Eucharistic mystery", even though "when they commemorate the Lord's Death and Resurrection in the Holy Supper, they profess that it signifies life in communion with Christ and they await his coming in glory". [121]

68.   The Decree does not overlook the spiritual life and its moral consequences: "The Christian way of life of these brethren is nourished by faith in Christ. It is strengthened by the grace of Baptism and the hearing of God's Word. This way of life expresses itself in private prayer, in meditation on the Bible, in Christian family life, and in services of worship offered by Communities assembled to praise God. Furthermore, their worship sometimes displays notable features of the ancient, common liturgy". [122]

The Council document moreover does not limit itself to these spiritual, moral and cultural aspects but extends its appreciation to the lively sense of justice and to the sincere charity towards others which are present among these brothers and sisters. Nor does it overlook their efforts to make social conditions more humane and to promote peace. All this is the result of a sincere desire to be faithful to the Word of Christ as the source of Christian life.

The text thus raises a series of questions which, in the area of ethics and morality, is be-

---

[121] *Ibid.*, 22.
[122] *Ibid.*, 23.

coming ever more urgent in our time: "There are many Christians who do not always understand the Gospel in the same way as Catholics".[123] In this vast area there is much room for dialogue concerning the moral principles of the Gospel and their implications.

69.   The hopes and invitation expressed by the Second Vatican Council have been acted upon, and bilateral theological dialogue with the various worldwide Churches and Christian Communities in the West has been progressively set in motion.

Moreover, with regard to multilateral dialogue, as early as 1964 the process of setting up a "Joint Working Group" with the World Council of Churches was begun, and since 1968 Catholic theologians have been admitted as full members of the theological Department of the Council, the Commission on Faith and Order.

This dialogue has been and continues to be fruitful and full of promise. The topics suggested by the Council Decree have already been addressed, or will be in the near future. The reflections of the various bilateral dialogues, conducted with a dedication which deserves the praise of all those committed to ecumenism, have concentrated on many disputed questions such as Baptism, the Eucharist, the ordained ministry, the sacramentality and authority of the Church and apostolic succession. As a result, unexpected possibilities for resolving these questions have come to

[123] *Ibid.*

80

light, while at the same time there has been a realization that certain questions need to be studied more deeply.

70.   This difficult and delicate research, which involves questions of faith and respect for one's own conscience as well as for the consciences of others, has been accompanied and sustained by the prayer of the Catholic Church and of the other Churches and Ecclesial Communities. Prayer for unity, already so deeply rooted in and spread throughout the body of the Church, shows that Christians do indeed see the importance of ecumenism. Precisely because the search for full unity requires believers to question one another in relation to their faith in the one Lord, prayer is the source of enlightenment concerning the truth which has to be accepted in its entirety.

Moreover, through prayer the quest for unity, far from being limited to a group of specialists, comes to be shared by all the baptized. Everyone, regardless of their role in the Church or level of education, can make a valuable contribution, in a hidden and profound way.

Ecclesial relations

71.   We must give thanks to Divine Providence also for all the events which attest to progress on the path to unity. Besides theological dialogue, mention should be made of other forms of encounter, common prayer and practical cooperation. Pope Paul VI strongly encouraged this pro-

cess by his visit to the headquarters of the World Council of Churches in Geneva on 10 June 1969, and by his many meetings with representatives of various Churches and Ecclesial Communities. Such contacts greatly help to improve mutual knowledge and to increase Christian fraternity.

Pope John Paul I, during his very brief Pontificate, expressed the desire to continue on this path.[124] The Lord has enabled me to carry on this work. In addition to important ecumenical meetings held in Rome, a significant part of my Pastoral Visits is regularly devoted to fostering Christian unity. Some of my journeys have a precise ecumenical "priority", especially in countries where the Catholic communities constitute a minority with respect to the post-Reformation communities or where the latter represent a considerable portion of the believers in Christ in a given society.

72. This is true above all for the European countries, in which these divisions first appeared, and for North America. In this regard, without wishing to minimize the other visits, I would especially mention those within Europe which took me twice to Germany, in November 1980 and in April-May 1987; to the United Kingdom (England, Scotland and Wales) in May-June 1982; to Switzerland in June 1984; and to the Scandinavian and Nordic countries (Finland, Sweden, Norway, Denmark and Iceland) in June 1989. In an atmo-

---

[124] Cf. Radio Message *Urbi et Orbi* (27 August 1978): *AAS* 70 (1978), 695-696.

sphere of joy, mutual respect, Christian solidarity and prayer I met so very many brothers and sisters, all making a committed effort to be faithful to the Gospel. Seeing all this has been for me a great source of encouragement. We experienced the Lord's presence among us.

In this respect I would like to mention one demonstration dictated by fraternal charity and marked by deep clarity of faith which made a profound impression on me. I am speaking of the Eucharistic celebrations at which I presided in Finland and Sweden during my journey to the Scandinavian and Nordic countries. At Communion time, the Lutheran Bishops approached the celebrant. They wished, by means of an agreed gesture, to demonstrate their desire for that time when we, Catholics and Lutherans, will be able to share the same Eucharist, and they wished to receive the celebrant's blessing. With love I blessed them. The same gesture, so rich in meaning, was repeated in Rome at the Mass at which I presided in Piazza Farnese, on the sixth centenary of the canonization of Saint Birgitta of Sweden, on 6 October 1991.

I have encountered similar sentiments on the other side of the ocean also: in Canada, in September 1984; and particularly in September 1987 in the United States, where one notices a great ecumenical openness. This was the case, to give one example, of the ecumenical meeting held at Columbia, South Carolina on 11 September 1987. The very fact that such meetings regularly take place between the Pope and these brothers and sisters whose Churches and Ecclesial Communities originate in the Reformation is important in itself. I am deeply grateful for the warm reception which I have received both from the leaders of the various Communities and from the Communities as a whole. From this standpoint, I consider significant the ecumenical celebration of the Word held in Columbia on the theme of the family.

73. It is also a source of great joy to observe how in the postconciliar period and in the local Churches many programmes and activities on behalf of Christian unity are in place, programmes and activities which have a stimulating effect at the level of Episcopal Conferences, individual Dioceses and parishes, and at the level of the various ecclesial organizations and movements.

Achievements of cooperation

74. "Not every one who says to me, 'Lord, Lord', will enter the kingdom of heaven, but he who does the will of my Father who is in heaven" (*Mt* 7:21). The consistency and honesty of intentions and of statements of principles are verified by their application to real life. The Council Decree on Ecumenism notes that among other Christians "the faith by which they believe in Christ bears fruit in praise and thanksgiving for the benefits received from the hands of God. Joined to it are a lively sense of justice and a true neighbourly charity".[125]

    [125] SECOND VATICAN ECUMENICAL COUNCIL, Decree on Ecumenism *Unitatis Redintegratio*, 23.

What has just been outlined is fertile ground not only for dialogue but also for practical cooperation: "Active faith has produced many organizations for the relief of spiritual and bodily distress, the education of youth, the advancement of humane social conditions, and the promotion of peace throughout the world".[126]

Social and cultural life offers ample opportunities for ecumenical cooperation. With increasing frequency Christians are working together to defend human dignity, to promote peace, to apply the Gospel to social life, to bring the Christian spirit to the world of science and of the arts. They find themselves ever more united in striving to meet the sufferings and the needs of our time: hunger, natural disasters and social injustice.

75.   For Christians, this cooperation, which draws its inspiration from the Gospel itself, is never mere humanitarian action. It has its reason for being in the Lord's words: "For I was hungry and you gave me food" (*Mt* 25:35). As I have already emphasized, the cooperation among Christians clearly manifests that degree of communion which already exists among them.[127]

Before the world, united action in society on the part of Christians has the clear value of a joint witness to the name of the Lord. It is also a form of proclamation, since it reveals the face of Christ.

The doctrinal disagreements which remain exercise a negative influence and even place limits

[126] *Ibid.*
[127] Cf. *ibid.*, 12.

on cooperation. Still, the communion of faith which already exists between Christians provides a solid foundation for their joint action not only in the social field but also in the religious sphere.

Such cooperation will facilitate the quest for unity. The Decree on Ecumenism noted that "through such cooperation, all believers in Christ are able to learn easily how they can understand each other better and esteem each other more, and how the road to the unity of Christians may be made smooth".[128]

76. In this context, how can I fail to mention the ecumenical interest in peace, expressed in prayer and action by ever greater numbers of Christians and with a steadily growing theological inspiration? It could not be otherwise. Do we not believe in Jesus Christ, the Prince of Peace? Christians are becoming ever more united in their rejection of violence, every kind of violence, from wars to social injustice.

We are called to make ever greater efforts, so that it may be ever more apparent that religious considerations are not the real cause of current conflicts, even though, unfortunately, there is still a risk of religion being exploited for political and polemical purposes.

In 1986, at Assisi, during the *World Day of Prayer for Peace*, Christians of the various Churches and Ecclesial Communities prayed with one voice to the Lord of history for peace in the

[128] *Ibid.*

world. That same day, in a different but parallel way, Jews and representatives of non-Christian religions also prayed for peace in a harmonious expression of feelings which struck a resonant chord deep in the human spirit.

Nor do I wish to overlook the *Day of Prayer for Peace in Europe, especially in the Balkans*, which took me back to the town of Saint Francis as a pilgrim on 9-10 January 1993, and the *Mass for Peace in the Balkans and especially in Bosnia-Hercegovina*, which I celebrated on 23 January 1994 in Saint Peter's Basilica during the *Week of Prayer for Christian Unity*.

When we survey the world joy fills our hearts. For we note that Christians feel ever more challenged by the issue of peace. They see it as intimately connected with the proclamation of the Gospel and with the coming of God's Kingdom.

CHAPTER III

QUANTA EST NOBIS VIA?

Continuing and deepening dialogue

77.   We can now ask how much further we must travel until that blessed day when full unity in faith will be attained and we can celebrate together in peace the Holy Eucharist of the Lord. The greater mutual understanding and the doctrinal convergences already achieved between us, which have resulted in an affective and effective growth of communion, cannot suffice for the conscience of Christians who profess that the Church is one, holy, catholic and apostolic. The ultimate goal of the ecumenical movement is to re-establish full visible unity among all the baptized.

In view of this goal, all the results so far attained are but one stage of the journey, however promising and positive.

78.   In the ecumenical movement, it is not only the Catholic Church and the Orthodox Churches which hold to this demanding concept of the unity willed by God. The orientation towards such unity is also expressed by others.[129]

---

[129] The steady work of the Commission on Faith and Order has led to a comparable vision adopted by the Seventh Assembly of the World Council of Churches in the Canberra Declaration (7-20 Feb-

Ecumenism implies that the Christian communities should help one another so that there may be truly present in them the full content and all the requirements of "the heritage handed down by the Apostles".[130] Without this, full communion will never be possible. This mutual help in the search for truth is a sublime form of evangelical charity.

The documents of the many International Mixed Commissions of dialogue have expressed this commitment to seeking unity. On the basis of a certain fundamental doctrinal unity, these texts discuss Baptism, Eucharist, ministry and authority.

From this basic but partial unity it is now necessary to advance towards the visible unity which is required and sufficient and which is manifested in a real and concrete way, so that the Churches may truly become a sign of that full communion in the one, holy, catholic and apostolic Church which will be expressed in the common celebration of the Eucharist.

This journey towards the necessary and sufficient visible unity, in the communion of the one Church willed by Christ, continues to require patient and courageous efforts. In this process, one must not impose any burden beyond that which is strictly necessary (cf. *Acts* 15:28).

79.   It is already possible to identify the areas in need of fuller study before a true consensus of faith can be achieved: 1) the relationship between Sacred Scripture, as the highest authority in matters of faith, and Sacred Tradition, as indispensable to the interpretation of the Word of God; 2) the Eucharist, as the Sacrament of the Body and Blood of Christ, an offering of praise to the Father, the sacrificial memorial and Real Presence of Christ and the sanctifying outpouring of the Holy Spirit; 3) Ordination, as a Sacrament, to the threefold ministry of the episcopate, presbyterate and diaconate; 4) the Magisterium of the Church, entrusted to the Pope and the Bishops in communion with him, understood as a responsibility and an authority exercised in the name of Christ for teaching and safeguarding the faith; 5) the Virgin Mary, as Mother of God and Icon of the Church, the spiritual Mother who intercedes for Christ's disciples and for all humanity.

In this courageous journey towards unity, the transparency and the prudence of faith require us to avoid both false irenicism and indifference to the Church's ordinances.[131] Conversely, that same transparency and prudence urge us to reject a halfhearted commitment to unity and, even more, a prejudicial opposition or a defeatism which tends to see everything in negative terms.

To uphold a vision of unity which takes account of all the demands of revealed truth does

[131] Cf. *ibid.*, 4 and 11.

not mean to put a brake on the ecumenical move-ment.[132] On the contrary, it means preventing it from settling for apparent solutions which would lead to no firm and solid results.[133] The obligation to respect the truth is absolute. Is this not the law of the Gospel?

Reception of the results already achieved

80.   While dialogue continues on new subjects or develops at deeper levels, a new task lies before us: that of receiving the results already achieved. These cannot remain the statements of bilateral commissions but must become a common heri-tage. For this to come about and for the bonds of communion to be thus strengthened, a serious ex-amination needs to be made, which, by different ways and means and at various levels of respon-sibility, must involve the whole People of God. We are in fact dealing with issues which fre-quently are matters of faith, and these require uni-versal consent, extending from the Bishops to the lay faithful, all of whom have received the anointing of the Holy Spirit.[134] It is the same Spirit who assists the Magisterium and awakens the *sensus fidei*.

Consequently, for the outcome of dialogue to be received, there is needed a broad and precise

---

[132] Cf. Address to the Cardinals and the Roman Curia (28 June 1985), 6: *AAS* 77 (1985), 1153.

[133] Cf. *ibid.*

[134] Cf. SECOND VATICAN ECUMENICAL COUNCIL, Dogmatic Constitution on the Church *Lumen Gentium*, 12.

critical process which analyzes the results and rigorously tests their consistency with the Tradition of faith received from the Apostles and lived out in the community of believers gathered around the Bishop, their legitimate Pastor.

81.   This process, which must be carried forward with prudence and in a spirit of faith, will be assisted by the Holy Spirit. If it is to be successful, its results must be made known in appropriate ways by competent persons. Significant in this regard is the contribution which theologians and faculties of theology are called to make by exercising their charism in the Church. It is also clear that ecumenical commissions have very specific responsibilities and tasks in this regard.

The whole process is followed and encouraged by the Bishops and the Holy See. The Church's teaching authority is responsible for expressing a definitive judgment.

In all this, it will be of great help methodologically to keep carefully in mind the distinction between the deposit of faith and the formulation in which it is expressed, as Pope John XXIII recommended in his opening address at the Second Vatican Council.[135]

Continuing spiritual ecumenism and bearing witness to holiness

82.   It is understandable how the seriousness of the commitment to ecumenism presents a deep

[135] Cf. *AAS* 54 (1962), 792.

challenge to the Catholic faithful. The Spirit calls them to make a serious examination of conscience. The Catholic Church must enter into what might be called a "dialogue of conversion", which constitutes the spiritual foundation of ecumenical dialogue. In this dialogue, which takes place before God, each individual must recognize his own faults, confess his sins and place himself in the hands of the One who is our Intercessor before the Father, Jesus Christ.

Certainly, in this attitude of conversion to the will of the Father and, at the same time, of repentance and absolute trust in the reconciling power of the truth which is Christ, we will find the strength needed to bring to a successful conclusion the long and arduous pilgrimage of ecumenism. The "dialogue of conversion" with the Father on the part of each Community, with the full acceptance of all that it demands, is the basis of fraternal relations which will be something more than a mere cordial understanding or external sociability. The bonds of fraternal *koinonia* must be forged before God and in Christ Jesus.

Only the act of placing ourselves before God can offer a solid basis for that conversion of individual Christians and for that constant reform of the Church, insofar as she is also a human and earthly institution,[136] which represent the preconditions for all ecumenical commitment. One of the first steps in ecumenical dialogue is the effort

[136] Cf. SECOND VATICAN ECUMENICAL COUNCIL, Decree on Ecumenism *Unitatis Redintegratio*, 6.

to draw the Christian Communities into this completely interior spiritual space in which Christ, by the power of the Spirit, leads them all, without exception, to examine themselves before the Father and to ask themselves whether they have been faithful to his plan for the Church.

83.   I have mentioned the will of the Father and the spiritual space in which each community hears the call to overcome the obstacles to unity. All Christian Communities know that, thanks to the power given by the Spirit, obeying that will and overcoming those obstacles are not beyond their reach. All of them in fact have martyrs for the Christian faith.[137] Despite the tragedy of our divisions, these brothers and sisters have preserved an attachment to Christ and to the Father so radical and absolute as to lead even to the shedding of blood. But is not this same attachment at the heart of what I have called a "dialogue of conversion"? Is it not precisely this dialogue which clearly shows the need for an ever more profound experience of the truth if full communion is to be attained?

84.   In a theocentric vision, we Christians already have a common *Martyrology*. This also includes the martyrs of our own century, more numerous than one might think, and it shows how, at a profound level, God preserves communion among the baptized in the supreme demand of

---

[137] Cf. *ibid.*, 4; PAUL VI, Homily for the Canonization of the Ugandan Martyrs (18 October 1964): *AAS* 56 (1964), 906.

faith, manifested in the sacrifice of life itself.[138] The fact that one can die for the faith shows that other demands of the faith can also be met. I have already remarked, and with deep joy, how an imperfect but real communion is preserved and is growing at many levels of ecclesial life. I now add that this communion is already perfect in what we all consider the highest point of the life of grace, *martyria* unto death, the truest communion possible with Christ who shed his Blood, and by that sacrifice brings near those who once were far off (cf. *Eph* 2:13).

While for all Christian communities the martyrs are the proof of the power of grace, they are not the only ones to bear witness to that power. Albeit in an invisible way, the communion between our Communities, even if still incomplete, is truly and solidly grounded in the full communion of the Saints—those who, at the end of a life faithful to grace, are in communion with Christ in glory. These *Saints* come from all the Churches and Ecclesial Communities which gave them entrance into the communion of salvation.

When we speak of a common heritage, we must acknowledge as part of it not only the institutions, rites, means of salvation and the traditions which all the communities have preserved and by which they have been shaped, but first and foremost this reality of holiness.[139]

---

[138] Cf. JOHN PAUL II, Apostolic Letter *Tertio Millennio Adveniente* (10 November 1994), 37: *AAS* 87 (1995), 29-30.

[139] Cf. PAUL VI, Address at the Shrine in Namugongo, Uganda (2 August 1969): *AAS* 61 (1969), 590-591.

In the radiance of the "heritage of the saints" belonging to all Communities, the "dialogue of conversion" towards full and visible unity thus appears as a source of hope. This universal presence of the Saints is in fact a proof of the transcendent power of the Spirit. It is the sign and proof of God's victory over the forces of evil which divide humanity. As the liturgies sing: "You are glorified in your Saints, for their glory is the crowning of your gifts".[140]

Where there is a sincere desire to follow Christ, the Spirit is often able to pour out his grace in extraordinary ways. The experience of ecumenism has enabled us to understand this better. If, in the interior spiritual space described above, Communities are able truly to "be converted" to the quest for full and visible communion, God will do for them what he did for their Saints. He will overcome the obstacles inherited from the past and will lead Communities along his paths to where he wills: to the visible *koinonia* which is both praise of his glory and service of his plan of salvation.

85.   Since God in his infinite mercy can always bring good even out of situations which are an offence to his plan, we can discover that the Spirit has allowed conflicts to serve in some circumstances to make explicit certain aspects of the Christian vocation, as happens in the lives of the Saints. In spite of fragmentation, which is an evil

---

[140] Cf. *Missale Romanum, Praefatio de Sanctis I:* Sanctorum "coronando merita tua dona coronans".

from which we need to be healed, there has resulted a kind of rich bestowal of grace which is meant to embellish the *koinonia*. God's grace will be with all those who, following the example of the Saints, commit themselves to meeting its demands. How can we hesitate to be converted to the Father's expectations? He is with us.

Contribution of the Catholic Church to the quest for Christian unity

86.   The Constitution *Lumen Gentium*, in a fundamental affirmation echoed by the Decree *Unitatis Redintegratio*,[141] states that the one Church of Christ subsists in the Catholic Church.[142] The Decree on Ecumenism emphasizes the presence in her of the fullness (*plenitudo*) of the means of salvation.[143] Full unity will come about when all share in the fullness of the means of salvation entrusted by Christ to his Church.

87.   Along the way that leads to full unity, ecumenical dialogue works to awaken a reciprocal fraternal assistance, whereby Communities strive to give in mutual exchange what each one needs in order to grow towards definitive fullness in accordance with God's plan (cf. *Eph* 4:11-13). I have said how we are aware, as the Catholic Church,

---

[141] Cf. SECOND VATICAN ECUMENICAL COUNCIL, Decree on Ecumenism *Unitatis Redintegratio*, 4.

[142] Cf. SECOND VATICAN ECUMENICAL COUNCIL, Dogmatic Constitution on the Church *Lumen Gentium*, 8.

[143] Cf. SECOND VATICAN ECUMENICAL COUNCIL, Decree on Ecumenism *Unitatis Redintegratio*, 3.

that we have received much from the witness borne by other Churches and Ecclesial Communities to certain common Christian values, from their study of those values, and even from the way in which they have emphasized and experienced them. Among the achievements of the last thirty years, this reciprocal fraternal influence has had an important place. At the stage which we have now reached,[144] this process of mutual enrichment must be taken seriously into account. Based on the communion which already exists as a result of the ecclesial elements present in the Christian communities, this process will certainly be a force impelling towards full and visible communion, the desired goal of the journey we are making. Here we have the ecumenical expression of the Gospel law of sharing. This leads me to state once more: "We must take every care to meet the legitimate desires and expectations of our Christian brethren, coming to know their way of thinking and their sensibilities ... The talents of each must be developed for the utility and the advantage of all".[145]

The ministry of unity of the Bishop of Rome

88.   Among all the Churches and Ecclesial Communities, the Catholic Church is conscious

---

[144] After the Lima Document of the Commission on Faith and Order, *Baptism, Eucharist and Ministry* (January 1982), and in the spirit of the Declaration of the Seventh General Assembly of the World Council of Churches, *The Unity of the Church as "koinonia": Gift and Task* (Canberra, 7-20 February 1991): cf. *Istina* 36 (1991), 389-391.

[145] Address to the Cardinals and the Roman Curia (28 June 1985), 4: *AAS* 77 (1985), 1151-1152.

that she has preserved the ministry of the Successor of the Apostle Peter, the Bishop of Rome, whom God established as her "perpetual and visible principle and foundation of unity" [146] and whom the Spirit sustains in order that he may enable all the others to share in this essential good. In the beautiful expression of Pope Saint Gregory the Great, my ministry is that of *servus servorum Dei*. This designation is the best possible safeguard against the risk of separating power (and in particular the primacy) from ministry. Such a separation would contradict the very meaning of power according to the Gospel: "I am among you as one who serves" (*Lk* 22:27), says our Lord Jesus Christ, the Head of the Church. On the other hand, as I acknowledged on the important occasion of a visit to the World Council of Churches in Geneva on 12 June 1984, the Catholic Church's conviction that in the ministry of the Bishop of Rome she has preserved, in fidelity to the Apostolic Tradition and the faith of the Fathers, the visible sign and guarantor of unity, constitutes a difficulty for most other Christians, whose memory is marked by certain painful recollections. To the extent that we are responsible for these, I join my Predecessor Paul VI in asking forgiveness. [147]

89.   It is nonetheless significant and encouraging that the question of the primacy of the Bishop

---

[146] SECOND VATICAN ECUMENICAL COUNCIL, Dogmatic Constitution on the Church *Lumen Gentium*, 23.

[147] Cf. Discourse at the Headquarters of the World Council of Churches, Geneva (12 June 1984), 2: *Insegnamenti* VII/1 (1984), 1686.

of Rome has now become a subject of study which is already under way or will be in the near future. It is likewise significant and encouraging that this question appears as an essential theme not only in the theological dialogues in which the Catholic Church is engaging with other Churches and Ecclesial Communities, but also more generally in the ecumenical movement as a whole. Recently the delegates to the Fifth World Assembly of the Commission on Faith and Order of the World Council of Churches, held in Santiago de Compostela, recommended that the Commission "begin a new study of the question of a universal ministry of Christian unity".[148] After centuries of bitter controversies, the other Churches and Ecclesial Communities are more and more taking a fresh look at this ministry of unity.[149]

90.   The Bishop of Rome is the Bishop of the Church which preserves the mark of the martyrdom of Peter and of Paul: "By a mysterious design of Providence it is at Rome that [Peter] con-

---

[148] WORLD CONFERENCE OF THE COMMISSION ON FAITH AND ORDER, Report of the Second Section, Santiago de Compostela (1993): *Confessing the One Faith to God's Glory*, 31, 2, Faith and Order Paper No. 166, World Council of Churches, Geneva, 1994, 243.

[149] To cite only a few examples: ANGLICAN-ROMAN CATHOLIC INTERNATIONAL COMMISSION, *Final Report*, ARCIC-I (September 1981); INTERNATIONAL COMMISSION FOR DIALOGUE BETWEEN THE DISCIPLES OF CHRIST AND THE ROMAN CATHOLIC CHURCH, *Report* (1981); ROMAN CATHOLIC/LUTHERAN JOINT COMMISSION, *The Ministry in the Church* (13 March 1981). The problem takes clear shape in the research conducted by the JOINT INTERNATIONAL COMMISSION FOR THE THEOLOGICAL DIALOGUE BETWEEN THE CATHOLIC CHURCH AND THE ORTHODOX CHURCH.

cludes his journey in following Jesus, and it is at
Rome that he gives his greatest proof of love and
fidelity. Likewise Paul, the Apostle of the Gentiles, gives his supreme witness at Rome. In this
way the Church of Rome became the Church of
Peter and of Paul".[150]

In the New Testament, the person of Peter
has an eminent place. In the first part of the Acts
of the Apostles, he appears as the leader and
spokesman of the Apostolic College described as
"Peter ... and the Eleven" (2:14; cf. 2:37, 5:29).
The place assigned to Peter is based on the words
of Christ himself, as they are recorded in the
Gospel traditions.

91.   The Gospel of Matthew gives a clear out-
line of the pastoral mission of Peter in the
Church: "Blessed are you, Simon Bar-Jona! For
flesh and blood has not revealed this to you, but
my Father who is in heaven. And I tell you, you
are Peter, and on this rock I will build my
Church and the powers of death shall not prevail
against it. I will give you the keys of the kingdom
of heaven, and whatever you bind on earth shall
be bound in heaven, and whatever you loose on
earth shall be loosed in heaven" (16:17-19). Luke
makes clear that Christ urged Peter to strengthen
his brethren, while at the same time reminding
him of his own human weakness and need of
conversion (cf. 22:31-32). It is just as though,
against the backdrop of Peter's human weakness,

[150] Address to the Cardinals and the Roman Curia (28 June 1985),
3: AAS 77 (1985), 1150.

it were made fully evident that his particular ministry in the Church derives altogether from grace. It is as though the Master especially concerned himself with Peter's conversion as a way of preparing him for the task he was about to give him in his Church, and for this reason was very strict with him. This same role of Peter, similarly linked with a realistic affirmation of his weakness, appears again in the Fourth Gospel: "Simon, son of John, do you love me more than these? ... Feed my sheep" (cf. *Jn* 21:15-19). It is also significant that according to the First Letter of Paul to the Corinthians the Risen Christ appears to Cephas and then to the Twelve (cf. 15:5).

It is important to note how the weakness of Peter and of Paul clearly shows that the Church is founded upon the infinite power of grace (cf. *Mt* 16:17; *2 Cor* 12:7-10). Peter, immediately after receiving his mission, is rebuked with unusual severity by Christ, who tells him: "You are a hindrance to me" (*Mt* 16:23). How can we fail to see that the mercy which Peter needs is related to the ministry of that mercy which he is the first to experience? And yet, Peter will deny Jesus three times. The Gospel of John emphasizes that Peter receives the charge of shepherding the flock on the occasion of a threefold profession of love (cf. 21:15-17), which corresponds to his threefold denial (cf. 13:38). Luke, for his part, in the words of Christ already quoted, words which the early tradition will concentrate upon in order to clarify the mission of Peter, insists on the fact that he will have to "strengthen his brethren when he has turned again" (cf. 22:32).

92.   As for Paul, he is able to end the description of his ministry with the amazing words which he had heard from the Lord himself: "My grace is sufficient for you, for my power is made perfect in weakness"; consequently, he can exclaim: "When I am weak, then I am strong" (2 *Cor* 12:9-10). This is a basic characteristic of the Christian experience.

As the heir to the mission of Peter in the Church, which has been made fruitful by the blood of the Princes of the Apostles, the Bishop of Rome exercises a ministry originating in the manifold mercy of God. This mercy converts hearts and pours forth the power of grace where the disciple experiences the bitter taste of his personal weakness and helplessness. The authority proper to this ministry is completely at the service of God's merciful plan and it must always be seen in this perspective. Its power is explained from this perspective.

93.   Associating himself with Peter's threefold profession of love, which corresponds to the earlier threefold denial, his Successor knows that he must be a sign of mercy. His is a ministry of mercy, born of an act of Christ's own mercy. This whole lesson of the Gospel must be constantly read anew, so that the exercise of the Petrine ministry may lose nothing of its authenticity and transparency.

The Church of God is called by Christ to manifest to a world ensnared by its sins and evil designs that, despite everything, God in his mercy can convert hearts to unity and enable them to enter into communion with him.

94.　　This service of unity, rooted in the action of divine mercy, is entrusted within the College of Bishops to one among those who have received from the Spirit the task, not of exercising power over the people—as the rulers of the Gentiles and their great men do (cf. *Mt* 20:25; *Mk* 10:42)—but of leading them towards peaceful pastures. This task can require the offering of one's own life (cf. *Jn* 10:11-18). Saint Augustine, after showing that Christ is "the one Shepherd, in whose unity all are one", goes on to exhort: "May all shepherds thus be one in the one Shepherd; may they let the one voice of the Shepherd be heard; may the sheep hear this voice and follow their Shepherd, not this shepherd or that, but the only one; in him may they all let one voice be heard and not a babble of voices ... the voice free of all division, purified of all heresy, that the sheep hear".[151] The mission of the Bishop of Rome within the College of all the Pastors consists precisely in "keeping watch" (*episkopein*), like a sentinel, so that, through the efforts of the Pastors, the true voice of Christ the Shepherd may be heard in all the particular Churches. In this way, in each of the particular Churches entrusted to those Pastors, the *una, sancta, catholica et apostolica Ecclesia* is made present. All the Churches are in full and visible com-

---

[151] *Sermon XLVI*, 30: CCL 41, 557.

munion, because all the Pastors are in communion with Peter and therefore united in Christ.

With the power and the authority without which such an office would be illusory, the Bishop of Rome must ensure the communion of all the Churches. For this reason, he is the first servant of unity. This primacy is exercised on various levels, including vigilance over the handing down of the Word, the celebration of the Liturgy and the Sacraments, the Church's mission, discipline and the Christian life. It is the responsibility of the Successor of Peter to recall the requirements of the common good of the Church, should anyone be tempted to overlook it in the pursuit of personal interests. He has the duty to admonish, to caution and to declare at times that this or that opinion being circulated is irreconcilable with the unity of faith. When circumstances require it, he speaks in the name of all the Pastors in communion with him. He can also—under very specific conditions clearly laid down by the First Vatican Council—declare *ex cathedra* that a certain doctrine belongs to the deposit of faith.[152] By thus bearing witness to the truth, he serves unity.

95.   All this however must always be done in communion. When the Catholic Church affirms that the office of the Bishop of Rome corresponds to the will of Christ, she does not separate this office from the mission entrusted to the whole body of Bishops, who are also "vicars and ambassadors

---

[152] Cf. FIRST VATICAN ECUMENICAL COUNCIL Dogmatic Constitution on the Church of Christ *Pastor Æternus: DS* 3074.

of Christ".[153] The Bishop of Rome is a member of the "College", and the Bishops are his brothers in the ministry.

Whatever relates to the unity of all Christian communities clearly forms part of the concerns of the primacy. As Bishop of Rome I am fully aware, as I have reaffirmed in the present Encyclical Letter, that Christ ardently desires the full and visible communion of all those Communities in which, by virtue of God's faithfulness, his Spirit dwells. I am convinced that I have a particular responsibility in this regard, above all in acknowledging the ecumenical aspirations of the majority of the Christian Communities and in heeding the request made of me to find a way of exercising the primacy which, while in no way renouncing what is essential to its mission, is nonetheless open to a new situation. For a whole millennium Christians were united in "a brotherly fraternal communion of faith and sacramental life ... If disagreements in belief and discipline arose among them, the Roman See acted by common consent as moderator".[154]

In this way the primacy exercised its office of unity. When addressing the Ecumenical Patriarch His Holiness Dimitrios I, I acknowledged my awareness that "for a great variety of reasons, and against the will of all concerned, what should have been a service sometimes manifested itself in a

---

[153] Second Vatican Ecumenical Council, Dogmatic Constitution on the Church *Lumen Gentium*, 27.

[154] Second Vatican Ecumenical Council, Decree on Ecumenism *Unitatis Redintegratio*, 14.

very different light. But ... it is out of a desire to obey the will of Christ truly that I recognize that as Bishop of Rome I am called to exercise that ministry ... I insistently pray the Holy Spirit to shine his light upon us, enlightening all the Pastors and theologians of our Churches, that we may seek—together, of course—the forms in which this ministry may accomplish a service of love recognized by all concerned".[155]

96.   This is an immense task, which we cannot refuse and which I cannot carry out by myself. Could not the real but imperfect communion existing between us persuade Church leaders and their theologians to engage with me in a patient and fraternal dialogue on this subject, a dialogue in which, leaving useless controversies behind, we could listen to one another, keeping before us only the will of Christ for his Church and allowing ourselves to be deeply moved by his plea "that they may all be one ... so that the world may believe that you have sent me" (*Jn* 17:21)?

The communion of all particular Churches with the Church of Rome: a necessary condition for unity

97.   The Catholic Church, both in her *praxis* and in her solemn documents, holds that the communion of the particular Churches with the Church of Rome, and of their Bishops with the

---

[155] Homily in the Vatican Basilica in the presence of Dimitrios I, Archbishop of Constantinople and Ecumenical Patriarch (6 December 1987), 3: *AAS* 80 (1988), 714.

Bishop of Rome, is—in God's plan—an essential requisite of full and visible communion. Indeed full communion, of which the Eucharist is the highest sacramental manifestation, needs to be visibly expressed in a ministry in which all the Bishops recognize that they are united in Christ and all the faithful find confirmation for their faith. The first part of the Acts of the Apostles presents Peter as the one who speaks in the name of the apostolic group and who serves the unity of the community—all the while respecting the authority of James, the head of the Church in Jerusalem. This function of Peter must continue in the Church so that under her sole Head, who is Jesus Christ, she may be visibly present in the world as the communion of all his disciples.

Do not many of those involved in ecumenism today feel a need for such a ministry? A ministry which presides in truth and love so that the ship—that beautiful symbol which the World Council of Churches has chosen as its emblem—will not be buffeted by the storms and will one day reach its haven.

Full unity and evangelization

98.   The ecumenical movement in our century, more than the ecumenical undertakings of past centuries, the importance of which must not however be underestimated, has been characterized by a missionary outlook. In the verse of John's Gospel which is ecumenism's inspiration and guiding motif—"that they may all be one ... so that the

world may believe that you have sent me" (*Jn* 17:21)—the phrase *that the world may believe* has been so strongly emphasized that at times we run the risk of forgetting that, in the mind of the Evangelist, unity is above all for the glory of the Father. At the same time it is obvious that the lack of unity among Christians contradicts the Truth which Christians have the mission to spread and, consequently, it gravely damages their witness. This was clearly understood and expressed by my Predecessor Pope Paul VI, in his Apostolic Exhortation *Evangelii Nuntiandi*: "As evangelizers, we must offer Christ's faithful not the image of people divided and separated by unedifying quarrels, but the image of people who are mature in faith and capable of finding a meeting-point beyond the real tensions, thanks to a shared, sincere and disinterested search for truth. Yes, the destiny of evangelization is certainly bound up with the witness of unity given by the Church ... At this point we wish to emphasize the sign of unity among all Christians as the way and instrument of evangelization. The division among Christians is a serious reality which impedes the very work of Christ". [156]

How indeed can we proclaim the Gospel of reconciliation without at the same time being committed to working for reconciliation between

[156] Apostolic Exhortation *Evangelii Nuntiandi* (8 December 1975), 77: *AAS* 68 (1976), 69; cf. SECOND VATICAN ECUMENICAL COUNCIL, Decree on Ecumenism *Unitatis Redintegratio*, 1; PONTIFICAL COUNCIL FOR PROMOTING CHRISTIAN UNITY, *Directory for the Application of Principles and Norms on Ecumenism* (25 March 1993), 205-209: *AAS* 85 (1993), 1112-1114.

Christians? However true it is that the Church, by the prompting of the Holy Spirit and with the promise of indefectibility, has preached and still preaches the Gospel to all nations, it is also true that she must face the difficulties which derive from the lack of unity. When non-believers meet missionaries who do not agree among themselves, even though they all appeal to Christ, will they be in a position to receive the true message? Will they not think that the Gospel is a cause of division, despite the fact that it is presented as the fundamental law of love?

99.   When I say that for me, as Bishop of Rome, the ecumenical task is "one of the pastoral priorities" of my Pontificate,[157] I think of the grave obstacle which the lack of unity represents for the proclamation of the Gospel. A Christian Community which believes in Christ and desires, with Gospel fervour, the salvation of mankind can hardly be closed to the promptings of the Holy Spirit, who leads all Christians towards full and visible unity. Here an imperative of charity is in question, an imperative which admits of no exception. Ecumenism is not only an internal question of the Christian Communities. It is a matter of the love which God has in Jesus Christ for all humanity; to stand in the way of this love is an offence against him and against his plan to gather all people in Christ. As Pope Paul VI wrote to the Ecumenical Patriarch Athenagoras I: "May the

[157] Address to the Cardinals and the Roman Curia (28 June 1985), 4: *AAS* 77 (1985), 1151.

Holy Spirit guide us along the way of reconciliation, so that the unity of our Churches may become an ever more radiant sign of hope and consolation for all mankind".[158]

[158] Letter of 13 January 1970: *Tomos Agapis,* Vatican-Phanar (1958-1970), Rome-Istanbul, 1971, pp. 610-611.

EXHORTATION

100.   In my recent Letter to the Bishops, clergy and faithful of the Catholic Church indicating the path to be followed towards the celebration of the *Great Jubilee of the Holy Year 2000*, I wrote that "the best preparation for the new millennium can only be expressed in a *renewed commitment to apply, as faithfully as possible, the teachings of Vatican II to the life of every individual and of the whole Church*".[159] The Second Vatican Council is the great beginning—the Advent as it were—of the journey leading us to the threshold of the Third Millennium. Given the importance which the Council attributed to the work of rebuilding Christian unity, and in this our age of grace for ecumenism, I thought it necessary to reaffirm the fundamental convictions which the Council impressed upon the consciousness of the Catholic Church, recalling them in the light of the progress subsequently made towards the full communion of all the baptized.

There is no doubt that the Holy Spirit is active in this endeavour and that he is leading the Church to the full realization of the Father's plan, in conformity with the will of Christ. This will was

[159] Apostolic Letter *Tertio Millennio Adveniente* (10 November 1994), 20: *AAS* 87 (1995), 17.

expressed with heartfelt urgency in the prayer which, according to the Fourth Gospel, he uttered at the moment when he entered upon the saving mystery of his Passover. Just as he did then, today too Christ calls everyone to renew their commitment to work for full and visible communion.

101.   I therefore exhort my Brothers in the Episcopate to be especially mindful of this commitment. The two *Codes of Canon Law* include among the responsibilities of the Bishop that of promoting the unity of all Christians by supporting all activities or initiatives undertaken for this purpose, in the awareness that the Church has this obligation from the will of Christ himself.[160] This is part of the episcopal mission and it is a duty which derives directly from fidelity to Christ, the Shepherd of the Church. Indeed all the faithful are asked by the Spirit of God to do everything possible to strengthen the bonds of communion between all Christians and to increase cooperation between Christ's followers: "Concern for restoring unity pertains to the whole Church, faithful and clergy alike. It extends to everyone according to the potential of each".[161]

102.   The power of God's Spirit gives growth and builds up the Church down the centuries. As the Church turns her gaze to the new millennium, she asks the Spirit for the grace to strengthen her

---

[160] Cf. *Code of Canon Law,* Canon 755; *Code of Canons of the Eastern Churches,* Canon 902.

[161] SECOND VATICAN ECUMENICAL COUNCIL, Decree on Ecumenism *Unitatis Redintegratio,* 5.

own unity and to make it grow towards full communion with other Christians.

How is the Church to obtain this grace? In the first place, through *prayer*. Prayer should always concern itself with the longing for unity, and as such is one of the basic forms of our love for Christ and for the Father who is rich in mercy. In this journey which we are undertaking with other Christians towards the new millennium prayer must occupy the first place.

How is she to obtain this grace? Through *giving thanks*, so that we do not present ourselves empty-handed at the appointed time: "Likewise the Spirit helps us in our weakness ... [and] intercedes for us with sighs too deep for words" (*Rom* 8:26), disposing us to ask God for what we need.

How is she to obtain this grace? Through *hope* in the Spirit, who can banish from us the painful memories of our separation. The Spirit is able to grant us clear-sightedness, strength and courage to take whatever steps are necessary, that our commitment may be ever more authentic.

And should we ask if all this is possible, the answer will always be yes. It is the same answer which Mary of Nazareth heard: with God nothing is impossible.

I am reminded of the words of Saint Cyprian's commentary on *the Lord's Prayer*, the prayer of every Christian: "God does not accept the sacrifice of a sower of disunion, but commands that he depart from the altar so that he may first be reconciled with his brother. For God can be appeased only by prayers that make peace. To God, the better offering is peace, brotherly concord and a people made one in the unity of the Father, Son and Holy Spirit".[162]

At the dawn of the new millennium, how can we not implore from the Lord, with renewed enthusiasm and a deeper awareness, the grace to prepare ourselves, together, to offer this *sacrifice of unity*?

103.   I, John Paul, *servus servorum Dei*, venture to make my own the words of the Apostle Paul, whose martyrdom, together with that of the Apostle Peter, has bequeathed to this See of Rome the splendour of its witness, and I say to you, the faithful of the Catholic Church, and to you, my brothers and sisters of the other Churches and Ecclesial Communities: *"Mend your ways, encourage one another, live in harmony, and the God of love and peace will be with you ... The grace of the Lord Jesus Christ and the love of God and the fellowship of the Holy Spirit be with you all"* (2 Cor 13:11,13).

Given in Rome, at Saint Peter's, on 25 May, the Solemnity of the Ascension of the Lord, in the year 1995, the seventeenth of my Pontificate.

Joannes Paulus PP. II

---

[162] *On the Lord's Prayer*, 23: CSEL 3, 284-285.